CAMBRIDGE LIBRARY COLLECTION

Books of enduring scholarly value

History

The books reissued in this series include accounts of historical events and movements by eye-witnesses and contemporaries, as well as landmark studies that assembled significant source materials or developed new historiographical methods. The series includes work in social, political and military history on a wide range of periods and regions, giving modern scholars ready access to influential publications of the past.

Blessed Giles of Assisi

One of the original disciples of Saint Francis, Blessed Giles of Assisi preached a message of poverty and penance throughout Italy, the Holy Land, and North Africa before turning to a life of contemplation. His *Life*, here edited and translated by Walter Seton, offers valuable perspectives on this devout man, who strove not just to follow but to embody the Franciscan Rule. Seton analyses the sources for the short and long versions of the *Life*, arguing influentially that the Short Life represents the earlier, more authentic recension. His 1918 edition was based upon a previously unnoticed version of the Short Life contained in Oxford, Bodleian Library, MS Canonici Misc. 528. Facing-page Latin and English make the text accessible to students and experts alike. A vital addition to Franciscan studies when first published, this important work is now available to a new generation of scholars.

T0382582

Cambridge University Press has long been a pioneer in the reissuing of out-of-print titles from its own backlist, producing digital reprints of books that are still sought after by scholars and students but could not be reprinted economically using traditional technology. The Cambridge Library Collection extends this activity to a wider range of books which are still of importance to researchers and professionals, either for the source material they contain, or as landmarks in the history of their academic discipline.

Drawing from the world-renowned collections in the Cambridge University Library, and guided by the advice of experts in each subject area, Cambridge University Press is using state-of-the-art scanning machines in its own Printing House to capture the content of each book selected for inclusion. The files are processed to give a consistently clear, crisp image, and the books finished to the high quality standard for which the Press is recognised around the world. The latest print-on-demand technology ensures that the books will remain available indefinitely, and that orders for single or multiple copies can quickly be supplied.

The Cambridge Library Collection will bring back to life books of enduring scholarly value (including out-of-copyright works originally issued by other publishers) across a wide range of disciplines in the humanities and social sciences and in science and technology.

Blessed Giles of Assisi

WALTER W. SETON

CAMBRIDGE UNIVERSITY PRESS

Cambridge, New York, Melbourne, Madrid, Cape Town, Singapore,
São Paolo, Delhi, Dubai, Tokyo

Published in the United States of America by Cambridge University Press, New York

www.cambridge.org
Information on this title: www.cambridge.org/9781108017596

© in this compilation Cambridge University Press 2010

This edition first published 1918
This digitally printed version 2010

ISBN 978-1-108-01759-6 Paperback

BRITISH
SOCIETY OF FRANCISCAN STUDIES

VOL. VIII.

List of Officers of the Society, 1918.

Hon. President :—

PAUL SABATIER.

Committee :—

A. G. LITTLE, *Chairman.*
Professor T. W. ARNOLD.
P. DESCOURS.
Rev. W. H. FRERE.
T. E. HARVEY, M.P.
C. L. KINGSFORD.
Professor W. P. KER.
E. MOON.
Very Rev. H. RASHDALL.
Rev. H. G. ROSEDALE.
Professor M. E. SADLER.
Miss E. GURNEY SALTER.
WALTER W. SETON.
Professor T. F. TOUT.

Hon. Secretary and Treasurer :—

Mr. PAUL DESCOURS, 65 Deauville Road, Clapham Park,
London, S.W.

BLESSED
GILES OF ASSISI

BY

WALTER W. SETON

Qui nescit orare non cognoscit Deum.
—ÆGIDIUS

MANCHESTER: THE UNIVERSITY PRESS

1918

CONTENTS.

BLESSED GILES OF ASSISI.

CHAPTER I.

THE CALL TO POVERTY.

*" Ille homo, beatus Franciscus, nunquam deberet nominari, quin homo prae gaudio lamberet labia sua ; tantum modo sibi defuit unum, scilicet corporis fortitudo ; si enim habuisset tale corpus, quale ego habeo, scilicet ita robustum, proculdubio totus mundus eum sequi minime potuisset."—*ÆGIDIUS.

" TELL the Perugians that the bells shall never ring for my canonisation, nor for any great miracles wrought by me." And yet, after the lapse of more than six centuries, it appears probable that these, the last recorded words of the humble Giles of Assisi, may be disproved, and he may be the first of the original disciples of Saint Francis of Assisi to receive the full honours of canonisation. From among the little group of simple-minded, single-hearted men who at the dawn of the thirteenth century were the first to receive the message of evangelical perfection and to cluster around St. Francis, it is almost invidious to point to any one as the most fascinating and attractive of those Knights of his Round Table, as the Saint himself called them. The "Little Flowers of St. Francis," now fortunately so well known to modern readers, has endeared them one and all to us : and each of them, Leo, Bernard, Juniper, Giles, has his own place in our affections. But Blessed Giles of Assisi might, if he had not been the humblest and most retiring of men, have claimed a place second to none among the apostolic founders of the movement, which stirred the dry bones of Western Christendom in the thirteenth century.

Blessed Giles of Assisi has hitherto been known in this country in two ways: by the chapters included in most editions of the " Little Flowers," which give episodes in his life which are very beautiful, but not perhaps all of unquestionable authenticity; and by his " Golden Sayings," which have been admirably translated into English and edited by Father Paschal Robinson, O.F.M. This work is a completely satisfactory edition of the " Golden Sayings," and those who are primarily interested in Blessed Giles on account of his ascetic philosophy and of the contribution which he made to the religious philosophy and to the literature of the Middle Ages may not need to go further afield. But others, to whom the human document is of even greater fascination, will want to know Blessed Giles himself. As far as the present writer is aware, there is as yet no critical version of the Life of Blessed Giles published in this country, nor any translation of his life into English. To combine as far as is practicable the critical and the popular—never an easy task—is the object of this work.

The impulse to study and then to write about Blessed Giles came from the chance consultation of the catalogue of the Canonici Manuscripts in the Bodleian Library, the finding of a hitherto unknown copy of the life in Cod. Misc. 528, and the investigation of that MS., which has formed the basis of this edition. It is impossible to make a careful study of the manuscript sources of the Life of Blessed Giles without becoming immersed in the many complex problems which are interwoven with one another in early Franciscan literature. To a number of these it will be necessary to allude: but it would be going far beyond the scope of this work to attempt to solve some of these problems, for the complete settlement of which we still are and perhaps always shall be without sufficient material. The primary aim will be to get at the most primitive version of the Life, to discuss the position of Brother Leo as its author, and to make the personality of Giles real and living to British readers. Giles first appears in the Franciscan story about two years after St. Francis himself had made the great surrender, and, deliberately choosing a life of poverty, had embarked upon that venture of faith which was to earn for him first the ridicule and contempt of his relatives and friends in Assisi, then the affectionate regard and esteem of the dwellers in the towns and villages of the Umbrian plain, and now the devotion of the Faithful throughout the world. " The day will come," said the young Francis when in prison bonds in Perugia in 1202, " when the world will fall down and pray to me." [1] The words have come true, but nothing seemed more unlikely at the time when Giles, hearing from his friends and kinsmen of the eccentric and fanatical son of the merchant Peter Bernardone, and of his two disciples, Bernard of Quintavalle and Peter Cathanius, resolved to throw in his lot with them. The chronicles are silent concerning the earlier life of Giles : we do not know whether he was younger than Francis or older, but we get some impression of him from Thomas of Celano's description : [2] " a simple, upright, God-fearing man, who for a long time, perfect in obedience, lived a holy and devout life, by the labour of his hands, giving us an example of solitary life and of holy contemplation ".

On 23rd April, the day of England's Patron Saint, St. George, Giles took his resolve to leave the world and seek out St. Francis and his two disciples. It is not easy to determine the year in which his conversion and that of Bernard and Peter took place. It is equally difficult to determine the year of his death : and the two events must be calculated, the one in relation to the other.

Some MSS. of the life contain no dates : others contain dates which cannot be taken without reserve. The version which we believe to be the most primitive at present known, contains no date either of his conversion or of his death : the longer version gives in most MSS. the date 1209 for his conversion and 1262 for his death.

This, however, is clear from the early narratives of the foundation of the Order, that the call of the first disciples

---

[1] " Adhuc sanctus adorabor per seculum totum," II Cel. i. 4.
[2] I Cel. x. 25.

was about a year before the journey of St. Francis and his followers to Rome for the approval of their primitive Rule by the Pope. There has been much controversy as to the year to which the approval of the First Rule should be assigned. It was either 1209 or 1210: and if that is so, the conversion of Giles took place either in 1208 or 1209. A strong argument for the later date, 1209, is reached in a somewhat indirect way. All the versions agree in recording that Giles died on the Vigil of the Feast of St. George, at the hour of the early morning office: in other words, early on 23rd April. Now his death occurred either in 1261 or 1262. The MSS. which contain a date say 1262. The year 1261 is extremely improbable, because in 1261 Easter Sunday fell on 24th April: that being so, the 23rd April, being Easter Eve, would certainly not have been observed that year as the Feast of St. George, and if Giles had died on 23rd April, 1261, it seems certain that reference would have been made to that date as Easter Eve. On this basis, admittedly not very conclusive, it appears best to accept the statement of the best MSS. of the Chronicle of XXIV Generals—that Giles died on St. George's Day, 23rd April, 1262. The same MSS. say that he died in the fifty-second year from his conversion, while the MSS. of the Short Life[1] (including the one here edited) speak of his death as occurring " when fifty-two years had been completed ".[2] It would thus appear that the conversion of Giles could not have taken place earlier than in 1209.

A confirmation of this date is found in the fact that all the MSS. agree in referring to the death of St. Francis (4th Oct., 1226) as having taken place in the eighteenth year of Giles' conversion, that is seventeen years before April, 1226: which again brings us to 1209.[3]

Rising early on the morning of St. George's Day, Giles

[1] For explanation of the terms Short Life and Long Life, see p. 28.

[2] It is not very apparent on what authority Father Paschal Robinson states that Giles lived fifty-three years in the Order. " Golden Sayings," p. xl.

[3] In the narrative which follows the conclusions reached on certain critical questions discussed in detail in later chapters are assumed.

betook himself first of all to the Church of St. George, now part of Santa Chiara; and, having heard Mass, he set out to find St. Francis.

Leaving Assisi by the East Gate, now known as the Porta Nuova, he made his way past San Damiano to the leper settlement of Rivo Torto, which stood on the main road running from Perugia through Spello to Foligno. It was at the cross-roads, where the track from San Damiano joined the main road, that Giles prayed for guidance in his search for the Portiuncula and for St. Francis. The Portiuncula, or as it was then called Sancta Maria, lay surrounded by woods a little off the highway in the direction of Perugia. Giles soon found his prayer answered, for at that very moment Francis himself, making his way to the wood for prayer, came to meet him. Giles fell down at his feet and begged to be allowed to join his company. The answer of Francis to his appeal shows his burning conviction of the dignity of the life to which he had himself been called and to which he was to call others. " A great gift it is, dearest brother, which the Lord hath given thee. If the Emperor were to come to Assisi and choose one from the city to be his knight or his chamberlain, many would there be who would fain be chosen. How much greater a gift oughtest thou to count it, that God hath chosen thee and called thee to His court ! " And with these words he raised Giles and took him to the little church hidden in the woods, and, calling Brother Bernard, said, " The Lord hath sent us a good brother ". Thus did Giles cast in his lot with the little poor man of Assisi and join himself to a movement which was destined to purge, even to save, the Church.

There was no delay in giving Giles the outward and visible sign of his new vocation, the plain habit of coarse brown cloth which has persisted for seven centuries as the distinctive garb of those of the Order who have most closely followed their Founder. Leaving their humble dwelling in the woods at Sancta Maria, Francis and Giles set out for Assisi, doubtless following the long dusty road which still leads from the Portiuncula up to the gate now known as

Porta San Pietro, though it is likely that at that time the lower part of the road was nothing but a track in the woods. That afternoon walk was to be the first test of the new disciple's resolve. A poor woman accosted Francis and begged an alms for the love of Christ, an appeal which Francis never could resist. Giles, who was of course still in his worldly attire, rose to the occasion. Scarcely had his master bidden him divide his mantle and give the poor woman a share, than he hastily removed his garment and gave her not half but the whole. Immediately Giles was filled with the keenest joy: by this outward act of renunciation he had won his spurs as a Knight of the Round Table.

CHAPTER II.

THE MISSIONARY JOURNEYS.

*" Quis magis meretur vadens ad sanctum Jacobum vel ad sanctum Jacobum
ostendens viam ? "*—ÆGIDIUS.

THE first year of Giles' life as a Friar was spent in close
association with St. Francis. It is difficult to know whether
to accept the account given by the compiler of the Long Life
and based upon the " Legend of the Three Companions," how
immediately after the reception of Giles, Francis and his new
follower set off on a tour in the March of Ancona. The
critical aspects of the matter are discussed later. It seems
probable that there were tours during the time following the
reception of Giles and while the number of Friars was still
but four; not exactly for public preaching, but for private
hand-to-hand work with individuals.[1] One of these may well
have been the occasion when Francis and Giles went on foot
to the March of Ancona. But wherever the incident is placed
in that first year, it is one of the most beautiful and characteristic episodes of early Franciscan days. Francis, who, as
the " Mirror of Perfection " tells us, used the French tongue
when carried away with the exuberance of his feelings, went
along singing aloud in French and praising God. Turning to
his wondering companion he said : " Our Order will be like
a fisherman, who casts his nets into the waters, catching a
great multitude of fishes : the big ones he choses out, but the
small he leaves in the water." Such optimism was a test of
the new disciple, seeing that at that time the Order numbered

[1] Anal. Franc., Tom. iii. p. 76. *" Licet autem Sanctus adhuc populo non
plene praedicaret."*

(7)

but four : but, recognising instinctively the spiritual genius of the man whom he was following, he wondered but believed and exhorted others to do the same.   And so they returned to the Portiuncula and rejoined Bernard and Peter.

Months passed, during which the band of followers was raised first to six by the reception of Sabbatino, Morico, and John of Capella, and a little later to seven when Philip the Long joined them.   It was then that the first regular preaching mission of the whole band was undertaken.   St. Francis called them together and exhorted them to go out two and two into the great world which lay outside Umbria, bidding them lead men to repentance by their lives rather than by precept.   His unconquerable spiritual optimism and his never-failing confidence in his mission were infectious and irresistible. And thus they went out, as he bade them ; and whenever they came to a Church or to a wayside Calvary, they bowed themselves, devoutly saying : "We adore Thee, O Christ, and bless Thy Name for all the churches which are in all the world, because by Thy holy Cross Thou hast redeemed the world".

This time Bernard of Quintavalle was the companion of Giles, and their goal was the shrine of St. James at Compostella, a renowned place of pilgrimage.   Probably it was the late autumn when they set out on their journey and the year was that of Giles' conversion, either 1208 or 1209.   We learn very little as to this journey in either of the lives of B. Giles : except that it was a time of intense hardship, when they suffered hunger, cold, thirst, and persecution.   But love of his fellow-men carried Giles through these experiences : meeting a poor man he wanted to give him his garment, but as he had only his one tunic, he could merely take off the hood and give it to him : and this he did, going himself for twenty-one days without a hood.

The " Legend of the Three Companions " helps to fill in the details of this pilgrimage.   For though the name of Giles is not mentioned in those paragraphs, it is clear that the account relates to Bernard's tour with Giles.   At any rate they reached

Florence and could find no one to give them shelter. One night they spent in the porch of a house, for the lady of the house mistrusting them and their errand, would not allow them to come inside. Next morning, after a night spent in the intense cold of a Northern Italian winter, Bernard and Giles betook themselves to Church to hear Mass : and the mistress of the house went to the same Church. While at Church the brothers were offered an alms by one Guido, but Bernard refused to receive it, explaining that they had given up all for the love of God. The lady, wondering at their refusal of the proferred alms and discovering how she had misjudged them, took Bernard and Giles into her house and entertained them hospitably for some days. One other incident is recorded concerning this pilgrimage. At Ficarollo, a small place on the Po between Mantua and Ferrara in the plain of Lombardy, a man called to Giles, who went to him expecting to receive an alms from him : but the man mocked him instead, by placing dice in his hand and inviting him to play. " The Lord forgive thee " was the reply of the humble, self-restraining Giles.

The records do not make it clear whether it was at the end of an agreed period or as a result of a divine interposition that the eight returned to Sancta Maria at the same time, but it would seem to have been early in 1210: the pilgrimage had occupied the winter of 1209-1210. Fr. Paschal Robinson and the Editors of the "Chronicle of XXIV. Generals" assign this visit to St. James at Compostella to the year 1212, i.e. after the journey to Rome for the approbation of the Rule : but this is difficult to maintain against the evidence of Thomas of Celano and of " The Three Companions ": especially the latter, which in dealing with the conditions of that time definitely states that "their band was not yet called an Order ".[1]

Both versions of the Life of B. Giles are silent as to the next great event in his career—the visit along with Francis and the ten other disciples to Rome : but there can be no doubt that he was then with them. The consensus of critical opinion

[1] " Three Comp." x. : " nondum enim Ordo eorum dicebatur Religio ".

assigns the visit to Rome to the summer of 1210. It is scarcely necessary to describe it in detail, both because Giles himself is not even mentioned in the whole story and because the visit to Rome is one of the episodes most familiar to all who care for the narrative of the early days of the Franciscan Order. It was the occasion of the meeting of two of the greatest but most widely different personalities of the thirteenth century— Innocent III and Francis. Suffice it to say that the earnestness, piety, simplicity, and utter conviction of his calling shown by Francis overcame the caution and statesmanship of one of the greatest men who has ever occupied the Papal throne and who, beneath his exalted rank as a spiritual and temporal potentate, was a lover of true religion and ardently anxious for the reform of the Church. Innocent and Francis understood each other : and Francis left Rome with the Papal approbation of his Primitive Rule and with the Papal authority to preach repentance. Before they left on their homeward journey, Giles, along with St. Francis and the other ten, received the small tonsure as authority to preach the word.

Leaving Rome, St. Francis with his little band, including Giles, made his way back by slow stages to Assisi, where he appears to have taken up his abode at or close to the leper settlement of Rivo Torto.

Some obscurity rests over the events of the next few years in the life of B. Giles. It is difficult to fix the order in which he undertook some more distant journeyings. The records agree in telling us that he made a pilgrimage to the Holy Land and also that he visited the well-known shrines of St. Michael the Archangel at Gargano and St. Nicholas at Bari. On the whole it seems likely that it was either on his way to the Holy Land or on his return journey that he visited the two shrines in Apulia. The Short Life, which for reasons to be discussed later may be regarded as the more primitive and authoritative, speaks of his visit to the two shrines first and of his pilgrimage to Jerusalem second ; the order is reversed in the Long Life. There can, however, be no doubt that Giles did visit the Holy Land and make his way to the Holy

Sepulchre and other spots of special veneration : and he appears to have taken a companion with him. So far as the records of the Order go, Giles and his companion were the first followers of St. Francis to carry the Gospel of Poverty to the Holy Land. They were delayed at Brindisi waiting for a ship to carry them over seas : and Giles with his usual humility did not hesitate to earn his daily bread by carrying water. So too on his way back he was delayed at a place which is not quite certain from the narrative, either " Achon " to be identified with S. Jean d'Acre in Syria, or Ancona : here also Giles was not ashamed to support himself by the sweat of his brow in most menial ways, making baskets of rushes or bearing the dead to the place of burial or carrying water for the townsfolk. During his pilgrimage to Monte Gargano and Bari, he carried his message of penitence to all whom he met, both men and women. These events occupied some part of the years from 1210 to 1214 ; but it is unsafe to be more precise than to assign them generally to that period. It was in all probability after his return from these wanderings far afield, that Giles in " the seventh year of his conversion," that is either in 1214 or 1215, went to the hermitage of Fabriano in the March of Ancona. Francis had set him at liberty to go wherever the Spirit led him, but Giles had no wish to be thus loosed from authority and besought Francis to send him to some place, because his spirit could find no rest in such freedom. And so he was sent to Fabriano. It is not easy to discover from the records how long Giles remained in the hermitage of Fabriano. The Long Life speaks of him as being there many years, and it seems likely that the stay at Fabriano occupied most of the time between 1215 and 1219, when he set out on his last missionary tour—to North Africa. It was in the quiet and seclusion of Fabriano that, in the words of his biographer, the hand of the Lord was over him ; the strong mystical and ascetic bent of Giles' character began then to manifest itself more and more clearly. He began to give himself to contemplation, and in the ecstasy of his soul to understand the secrets of the spiritual world. It was in the hermitage of Fabriano, too, that he began to feel himself in a special way the butt of the assaults and persecutions of the Devil, and in the distress of his spiritual conflict he sought the help of St. Francis, asking him whether there were anything so terrible that it could not be borne while one said a single Paternoster : to which St. Francis answered that so terrible was the Devil, that one could not bear his assaults even for so long as it took to say half a Paternoster. It may have been at some time during these years that he was in the Church of Saint Apollinaris at Spoleto, when one night as he prayed he felt the malignant Presence threatening him and was freed only by dragging himself to the stoup of holy water and making the sign of the Cross.

A characteristic story is told of Giles during his sojourn at Fabriano. Burdened with the conviction of his own sinfulness, he went into a wood, and having called a boy brother to him he stripped himself naked and bade the boy drag him by a rope round his neck to the abode of the Brothers. " Have pity on me, my Brothers, on me sinful as I am ! " he exclaimed to the astonished Brothers : and as they implored him to reclothe himself, he continued : " I am not worthy to be a Brother Minor : but if ye desire to give me back my tunic out of compassion and as an alms, I receive it though unworthy ".

Yet once again the call of the Mohammedan world was to stir Giles out of his life of contemplation and send him forth to preach. According to Wadding it was in 1219 at the second General Chapter that St. Francis resolved to send out Friars to the Saracens and other infidels. To the lot of Giles it fell to go to Tunis in North Africa. His mission does not appear to have been a very successful one : he and his companions were met with fierce opposition on the part of the fanatical Moors ; and the Christian inhabitants, who evidently feared that they were being endangered by the Friars, who insisted on preaching to the Moors from the ship, compelled them to abandon their mission and return to Italy.

It is difficult to know at what period in B. Giles' life to place his stay in Rome described by the compiler of the

"Chronicle of the XXIV Generals". It is noteworthy that the narrative does not find confirmation either in the Short Life or in any early sources: but there is no special reason for questioning its authenticity. The most likely period to which to assign this second visit to Rome is between 1210 and 1214. We are told that he lived while in Rome in the monastery of the "Sanctorum Quatuor Coronatorum," of which nothing is known: but if the Friars had then been established, as they were in 1212, in the building in Trastevere, it might be supposed that Giles would have lived there. On this assumption—a rather slender one—it might even be argued that his visit to Rome was between 1210 and 1212. Of his life in the great city we know little, except that he lived entirely by the labour of his hands. At one time he would support himself by carrying logs of wood: at another he would lend a hand with getting in the harvest or gathering the vintage or shaking down the nuts from the trees. For all these varied services he would not receive payment in money, but only in kind, just sufficient to meet his bodily needs. A beautiful story is told, illustrating his sincerity and love of his fellow-men, which endeared him to all. He was fetching water for the monastery from the fountain, and on his way back with his water-pot well filled, was accosted by a stranger who asked for a drink. Giles refused, saying: "How can I give thee a drink and carry back what is left over for the monks?" The stranger, much annoyed, assailed him with abuse: but the long-suffering Giles took his water-pot to the monastery, fetched another water-pot full of water from the fountain, and took it to the house of the man, bidding him drink.

The return of Giles from his missionary journey to Tunis in 1219 or possibly 1220 closes a chapter in his career: his active ministry was at an end: for the rest of his long life we find him first in one place and then in another, but never very far from Assisi, the original home of the Order.

CHAPTER III.

THE LIFE OF CONTEMPLATION.

" Contemplatio est ignis, vnctio, ecstasis, gustus, requies, gloria."—Ægidius.

FOR ten years Giles had lived the active life of the missionary, with periods of retreat at Fabriano and doubtless elsewhere. Before him lay forty-two years to be spent mainly living the Religious life, generally in seclusion but often too in close and inspiring contact with the early leaders of the Order. Those years were not eventful so far as Giles was concerned : the actual incidents recorded about them are comparatively few.

When B. Giles first turned his back upon the world and found a spiritual leader in St. Francis, Bernard of Quintavalle was the first brother whom he met. Throughout the whole of St. Francis' career, these two—Bernard and Giles—were closely linked together by the bond of a complete mutual understanding and of a community of experience. It is quite what might be expected to find them meeting once again beside the death-bed of the master. The "Speculum Perfectionis" gives a touching account of this meeting. The dying Francis bethinks him of his first follower Bernard, who had had the courage to believe in him and to join him when he was alone, and he sends for him. Seating himself beside the couch on which the Saint lay, Bernard appealed to him for a blessing : " My father, I pray thee to bless me and show thy love for me, since if thou dost show thy fatherly love for me, I believe that God Himself and all the brothers will love me the more ". Blessed Francis could not see him, for many days before the light had faded from his eyes : but stretching out his right hand, he laid it on the head of Brother Giles, thinking to place it on the head of Brother Bernard who was sitting next to him. Immediately the inspiration of the Holy Ghost revealed to him his mistake and Brother Bernard came nearer and received the much coveted blessing.

Thus did B. Giles watch by the death-bed of the man who had called him from the world and directed his life into new channels. Broken-hearted, we may well believe, by the bereavement which he had suffered, he left the Portiuncula with one companion, Gratian, and betook himself to the wild district of Cetona in Tuscany, not far from Chiusi, to the Convent of Cibbotola, to spend the Lent of St. Martin. It was during his stay at Cetona that in his sleep he had a vision of Blessed Francis himself. This experience, followed by days of prayer and fasting, was to lead up to an even greater crisis in his spiritual life; for three days before Christmas he had a vision of Jesus Christ manifest before his eyes. Just as St. Francis himself at the end of his observance of the Lent of St. Michael on Mount Alverna reached the climax of his spiritual career in the vision of the crucified Seraph and the receiving of the Sacred Wounds, so B. Giles found in his experiences at Cetona an objective revelation of his Lord which remained with him throughout the remainder of his life. From that time the contemplative bent which had already shown itself at Fabriano or even earlier, became the dominant characteristic of his life and character.

In no way was Giles a more loyal follower of St. Francis than in his zeal for the Lady Poverty: it was for him and for St. Clare and others of the earliest followers to hand on the torch lighted by the Saint, and to resist by word and deed the influences which Elias of Cortona and his followers were ever seeking to introduce. The story of Brother Leo and the building of the great Church of San Francesco is well known, and from its evident connection with Leo himself, is one of the stories about Giles most clearly marked with authenticity. Elias, who undoubtedly possessed a very genuine loyalty to the person of St. Francis, coupled with much ambition and much disagreement with the Saint's ideals, set to work almost immediately after his canonisation in 1228 to collect funds for the erection of the great Church on the Colle d'Inferno and set up a marble urn to receive the alms of the Faithful.   Leo went and told Giles of this wanton departure from the life of Poverty, and Giles weeping replied : " If the building were as long as from here to Assisi, one small corner were enough for me to sojourn in," and turning to Leo he said : " If thou art a dead man, go and break that marble vase, which has been set up contrary to Holy Poverty to receive gifts of money : but if thou art alive, desist, for thou canst ill bare the tribulations of that Elias ! "   Whereupon Leo and a few other brothers as simple-hearted and courageous as himself went and smashed the porphyry urn and were chastised by the Minister-General, Elias.

Later on Giles out of devotion to St. Francis went to revisit Assisi and was taken to see the great Convent which had been built up adjoining San Francesco.   Turning to the Friars who lived there, he said with his caustic wit : " I tell you, my brothers, there is but one thing ye lack here, wives ! " and added, " Ye know well, that having thus discarded poverty, ye can easily discard chastity ".

Nearly twenty years had passed since Giles and Bernard had met beside the death-bed of their much-loved master. Once again they met at a death-bed, but this time it was Bernard who was dying.   Entering the sick man's chamber, Giles greeted his old friend and brother-in-arms with cheerful words, " Sursum corda, Brother Bernard, sursum corda ! " And Bernard, whose thoughts doubtless travelled back to that spring day in 1209 when St. Francis had brought to him the new brother whom the Lord had sent, full of joy bade the brothers prepare a place in which Giles could devote himself according to his wont to contemplation.   After partaking of a meal along with the brothers who stood around his couch, after exhorting them to love one another, and after telling them all that not for a thousand worlds would he have lost the privilege of serving Christ, this first disciple of the Order passed to his rest.

Giles will ever live in the affection of those who care for the beginnings of the Franciscan Order rather by his life and character than by any actual deeds. Many stories are told of him, mostly relating to the years of contemplative life. Most of them help to show the essential simplicity of his character and his deep religious nature: his profound humility and invariable submission to authority: but many of them also show how intensely human Giles was and remained in spite of his spiritual experiences.

One of the best-known stories relates to his preaching before St. Clare. It was at San Damiano, and an English Friar, a Master of Sacred Theology, was preaching before the Sisters. Before he had got very far with' his sermon, B. Giles interrupted him, saying: " Hold thy peace, Master, for I desire to preach ". The Master in all humility ceased preaching and Giles preached instead. When Giles had finished he allowed the Master to complete his interrupted sermon. St. Clare was greatly edified by the humility of the Master of Theology, because he had thus allowed himself to be interrupted by a lay brother.

B. Giles was never destitute of a sense of humour, even in the most sacred things. A brother came jubilant to him to tell him that he had had a vision of Hell and had seen not a single Friar Minor there. " I believe thee, my son," answered Giles. The brother, evidently feeling some doubt, said: " How is it, thinkest thou, my Father, that there is no Friar Minor in Hell; or how is it that I saw them not?" " Thou sawest none, my son," replied Giles, " because thou didst not descend deep enough, to that place where the wretches are tormented who have worn the habit of Friars Minor but have not done the works of such or observed the Rule !"

One of the most beautiful stories, illustrating the simplicity and directness of Giles' faith, is the one telling how he removed from the mind of a Brother Preacher doubt concerning the virginity of Our Lady. It is true that the story is one which is sometimes regarded as an interpolation in the narrative, but its beauty justifies the quoting of it and the question whether it can be historically defended seems scarcely relevant. A noted Brother Preacher had doubt as to the virginity of Our Lady and came for spiritual guidance to Giles. Before he had made known his doubt, Giles perceived it and going to meet him, struck on the ground with the stick which he carried, saying, "O Brother Preacher, a Virgin before birth!" and where he struck the ground, a most beautiful lily sprang up. And striking the ground again, he said, "O Brother Preacher, a Virgin in birth!" and a second lily sprang up. And striking yet a third time he said: "O Brother Preacher, a Virgin after birth!" and a third lily sprang up. And Giles then ran away, but the Brother Preacher was freed from his doubts.

No incident recorded concerning B. Giles has been more criticised on historical grounds than the one found in the "Chronicle of the XXIV Generals," and in the "Little Flowers," describing the visit of St. Louis, King of France, to B. Giles at Perugia. It is told how the holy monarch went as an unknown pilgrim with but few companions to the place where Giles abode. Giles immediately knew by divine inspiration who his visitor was, and the two met and embraced each other and remained for some time thus : at last St. Louis departed, without either having addressed a single word to the other. The brothers remonstrated with Giles for having allowed St. Louis to go, without saying a word to him, although St. Louis had come expressly to see him and hear him. But Giles answered them thus : "Dearest brothers, marvel not, if he spake nought to me nor I to him ; for as soon as we embraced each other, the light of divine wisdom revealed his heart to me and mine to him, and whatsoever he had thought to say to me and I to him, we heard better without the sound of words or lips or tongue than if we had conversed with our lips. And had we desired to explain by means of the voice those things which we felt within ourselves, our speech would have tended rather to desolation than to consolation. Wherefore be ye sure that the king went away marvellously comforted."

B. Giles, as one of the early disciples who had gone about with the Founder of the Order and had close personal touch with him, was, during his long years of contemplative retirement, visited by leading men among the Franciscans, and among others by St. Bonaventura, the Minister-General. To him Giles, with his genuine self-depreciation and humility, once said : " My Father, great grace has been given thee of God. But as for us, simple and ignorant folk, what can we do to be saved?" The General answered : "If God hath given to any man no grace save that he can love Him, that is enough ". " Can an unlearned man," asked Giles, " love God just as much as one instructed in letters?" " An old woman can love God more than a Master of Theology," answered Bonaventura. And Giles, carried away with fervour and zeal went to the garden wall, and seeing an old woman called out to her : " Poor little old woman, simple and unlearned, thou canst love the Lord thy God and be greater than Brother Bonaventura ". The story is characteristic of the two men and rings true. It is Bonaventura of whom the story is told how when the Papal envoy came to bring him the Cardinal's Hat and found him at his work in the kitchen, the saintly General merely answered, " Hang it up outside ! "

And it was Giles who watching with no small concern and distrust the growing tendencies towards book-learning in the Order and the departure from the primitive Franciscan simplicity, uttered the words of warning wrung from his anxious heart : "O Paris, Paris, thou art ruining the Order of St. Francis ! "

Reference has already been made to Cetona as the place where B. Giles found the climax of his spiritual experience in a vision of his Lord. But it is in no way inconsistent with all that is known of his life and character, to find Cetona likewise the scene of an incident simple, natural, mundane which revealed how intensely human Giles could be. He had made at Cetona a small garden where he had grown most excellent cabbages ; and while he was standing in the garden with a stick in his hand saying the Our Father, another brother came, just to test him, and began to cut down the cabbages with a sword and destroy them.   It was too much for the patience even of Giles : he rushed upon him and unceremoniously bundled him out of the garden.   The brother turned to him saying, " O brother Giles, where is thy patience and holiness? "   And Giles, with a sigh answered, " Forgive me, brother, for thou camest upon me unawares and I was unarmed and could not arm myself thus suddenly ".

CHAPTER IV.

THE LAST DAYS NEAR PERUGIA.

" Ego nolo mori meliori morte quam de contemplatione."—ÆGIDIUS.

THE lack of chronological setting in both the standard Lives of B. Giles makes it difficult to be sure when it was that he settled down in the Convent of Monteripido, not far from Perugia. A good many references to his life in that Convent are found, especially in the Long Life, and it seems likely that with increasing age and failing powers Giles remained during the last years of his life, possibly even from about 1234, very much in seclusion at Monteripido. He must have been a much revered figure in the Order, for he was one of the few remaining links with the old days, the days when the personality of St. Francis had kept the Order together as one family before the lamentable strife between the Spiritual friars and the Community began. He had seen the leading personalities in the Order pass away, Peter Cathanius in 1221, St. Francis himself in 1226, Bernard of Quintavalle about 1242, St. Clare in 1253 : most of the other early followers also had gone to their rest : and Giles was left—one of the last of the apostolic band —living, one may suppose, very much in the memory of past days, but with an unwavering hold upon the ideals which had taken possession of his life in 1209. He had yielded himself so completely to the life of contemplation and to the care of spiritual things, that the affairs of earth had almost ceased to concern him. It was sufficient to speak with him of the divine glory and sweetness of Paradise for him to go into an ecstasy immediately and remain for a long while unconscious and wrapped in the heavenly vision. So dominating a habit did this become that at times mischievous boys would call out to him the words Paradise, Paradise, just to have the satisfaction of seeing the saintly old man go into a trance. But these spiritual experiences, which might easily have caused a lesser man to swell with pride, only increased the native humility of B. Giles.   Hearing of some who had risen to exalted places in the world and had then fallen, he would say, " Let me lie on the ground, for if I do not rise, I shall not be able to fall ! "   On one occasion, between 1234 and 1236, Pope Gregory IX while at Perugia summoned Giles to his presence and Giles went, not without fear lest he should fall into an ecstasy in the presence of the Pope.   As soon as he began to converse with the Pope, he fell into an ecstasy, and the Pope, having seen for himself what he had already heard by repute, said to him :   " If thou diest before me, I will expect no other sign of thee, but will inscribe thy name in the catalogue of the Saints ".

The end came in 1262 in the Convent of Monteripido, and the desire which he had himself expressed to die not a death of martyrdom but one of contemplation was to be fulfilled. Enfeebled by old age and by the privations to which he had up to the last exposed his body, he fell into an acute fever and was tormented with cough and headache, so that he could neither eat nor sleep.   The devoted brothers of the Convent did all they could to relieve the sufferings of their dying master.   Meanwhile, the news of his impending death had spread to Perugia, and the Perugians knowing that he had himself expressed his longing that his bones should be laid at rest in the Portiuncula at Saint Mary of the Angels, sent bodies of armed men to keep guard, lest when the breath had left his body the precious remains should be carried away elsewhere and Perugia robbed of a venerated relic.   News of their somewhat aggressive devotion reached the dying man, and he said : " Tell the Perugians that the bells shall never ring for my canonisation, nor for any great miracles wrought by me : there shall be no sign given unto them save the sign of the prophet Jonas ".   And the Perugians hearing this answered : " Even though he be not canonised, we will have him ".   The remains of B. Giles were carried to Perugia and buried in the Church of San Francesco.   His dying words concerning the sign of the prophet Jonas found an unexpected fulfilment : for the Perugians, looking for a suitable stone from which to make his tomb, found a marble block upon which the story of Jonah was sculptured.   This they used for the tomb of B. Giles, believing it to be the fulfilment of his prophetic words and conclusive proof of his holiness.

CHAPTER V

SOURCES FOR THE LIFE OF BLESSED GILES.

THE sources for the Life of Blessed Giles may be divided roughly into two main classes. There are the accounts of him and references to him in manuscripts dealing with other subjects : and there are the manuscripts containing more or less complete and connected versions of his Life. It will be simplest to deal first with the former class, and to do so in the generally accepted order of date of composition.

[1230.] I. The LEGENDA PRIMA or First Life of St. Francis, written by THOMAS OF CELANO at the direction of Pope Gregory IX, at some date between the Saint's canonisation in 1228 and 25 May, 1230, contains the earliest account of the conversion of Giles and of his joining himself to St. Francis. It is only a matter of a few lines and the reference is I Cel. x. 25.[1]

Hunc vero, post non multum temporis, sequitur frater Ægidius, vir simplex et rectus ac timens Deum, qui longo tempore durans sancte, iuste ac pie vivendo, perfectae obedientiae, laboris quoque manuum, vitae solitariae, sanctaeque contemplationis nobis exempla reliquit.

One further brief reference to him occurs in I Cel. xii. 30, where, speaking of the missionary journey undertaken by St. Francis and his seven companions, he mentions how B. Giles and Bernard made their way to the shrine of Saint James at Compostella :—

Tunc frater Bernardus cum fratre Ægidio versus Sanctum Iacobum iter arripuit.

[1244.] II. The LEGEND OF THE THREE COMPANIONS.—

---

[1] P. Eduard d'Alençon's edition, 1906, p. 27.

(24)

This work, usually attributed to Brothers Leo, Angelo, and Ruffino, and believed to have been composed by them from their personal recollections of the Saint as a result of a direction of the General Chapter of 1244, gives in chapter ix.[1] a fuller account of B. Giles' admission to the band of followers than that of Thomas of Celano : and it describes his first missionary expedition along with St. Francis to the March of Ancona.

In chapter xii. [2] a list of the first twelve members of the Order of Friars Minor is given, in which B. Giles stands fourth.

[1263.] III. The LEGENDA MAJOR of ST. BONAVENTURE, which was completed by the date of the Chapter of the Order in 1263, and was based largely upon the work of Thomas of Celano and other early documents. Bonaventure refers in chapter iii., § 4, to the conversion of Giles, as the third disciple : he speaks of him as a simple and unlearned man who was frequently in divine ecstasies. Moreover, Bonaventure claims to have known Giles himself " *ego ipse oculata fide conspexi* ".

[1282.] IV. The CHRONICA of BROTHER SALIMBENE OF PARMA, written *circa* 1282-1287, contains one fact of prime importance, viz. that Brother Leo was the author of a Life of B. Giles : [3]

" *Fratris Ægidii vitam frater Leo, qui fuit unus de tribus specialibus sociis beati Francisci, sufficienter descripsit.*"

[1290.] V. BERNARD OF BESSA'S " DE LAUDIBUS SANCTI FRANCISCI ".[4] Bernard was Secretary of St. Bonaventure and thus had access to early, even contemporary sources. He wrote his work between 1270 and 1290. He again refers to B. Giles as the third disciple : " *tertius, frater Ægidius, vir admirabilis sanctitatis, cui pro gratia dicitur esse concessum a Domino, ut in his quae ad bonum animae pertinent, efficaciter adiuvet invocatus*".

[1318.] VI. SPECULUM PERFECTIONIS, a compilation which was certainly in existence in its present form in 1318,

---

[1] Edition of Marcellino da Civezza and Teofilo Domenichelli, 1899, p. 56. But it must be remembered that the authenticity of this fragmentary work is open to much doubt.

[2] *Ibid.*, p. 78.   [3] Chronica, Parma, 1857, p. 323.

[4] Analecta Franciscana, Tom. iii. p. 667.

that being the date stated by the earliest known MS. (the Mazarine MS.); it is probably based to a large extent upon the writings of the first companions, even though it would be unsafe to assert that the work in its present form is their writing.   It is, however, an early document of undoubted authority.   Chapter 36[1] mentions the reception of B. Giles *" apud Rigum Tortum,"* and describes the incident of his giving his cloak, at St. Francis' bidding, to a poor man.   In Chapter 85[2] it is related how St. Francis, describing the qualities of the ideal Friar Minor, said that he should possess *"mentem elevatam in contemplatione quam frater Ægidius habuit usque ad summam perfectionem "*.   Again, in Chapter 107[3] there is the pathetic story, how the dying Francis, wishing to give a last charge concerning the honour due to Brother Bernard, stretched out his right hand to place it on the head of Bernard, but being blind placed it instead on that of Giles, and immediately discovered his mistake through the Holy Spirit.

[1318-1328.]   VII.   The ACTUS BEATI FRANCISCI ET SOCIORUM EJUS.   This important compilation, which may be dated between 1318-1328, and which contains a portion of the hypothecated *Floretum* or source of the "Little Flowers," has preserved the four chapters,[4] Nos. 44 (*Qualiter domina Jacoba de Septem Soliis visitavit fratrem Ægidium*), 45 (*Quomodo dicente fratre Ægidio virgo ante partum, virgo in partu, virgo post partum, orta sunt tria lilia*), 46 (*De mirabili revelatione facta in cordibus sancti fratris Ægidii et sancti Ludovici regis Franciae*), and 47 (*De quodam mirabili consilio quod dedit frater Ægidius fratri Jacobo habenti gratiam raptus*), which on account of their questioned authenticity need special consideration, and of which Chapter 46 passed on intact into the "Little Flowers," where it appears as Chapter 34.

In addition to these four chapters the ACTUS gives us also several minor references of value : his being caught up to the third heaven (Chap. 1 ; 5): his words of cheer to the dying Brother Bernard (Chap. 5 ; 18): his presence when the angel

---

[1] Sabatier's edition, Paris, 1898, p. 67.   [2] *Ibid.*, p. 168.
[3] *Ibid.*, p. 212.   [4] Sabatier, *Actus B. Franc.*, 1902, pp. 138-145.

appeared to Brother Bernard (Chap 3 ; 6, 32): his words concerning Brother Bernard that not to all was the gift given by God as to Bernard, to feed himself on the wing like a swallow (Chap. 30; 10).

[1369.] VIII. The CHRONICA XXIV GENERALIUM, believed to have been composed before 1369 by Brother Arnold of Serrano, contains—apart from the complete Life of B. Giles—the following incidental references :—

(*a*) In the life of St. Francis :—[1]

"*Et post viii dies quidam vir de Assisio, Ægidius nomine, horum exemplo provocatus, in die sancti Georgii, cum omnia sua pauperibus erogasset, fuit sancto Patri habitu et religione coniunctus.*"

There is also the incident of B. Giles' advice to Leo as to the vase in which Elias collected subscriptions for building San Francesco.[2]

(*b*) In the life of Bernard of Quintavalle, there is the story of the dying saint placing his right hand on the head of B. Giles :[3] and again the story of B. Giles visiting the dying Bernard and encouraging him with his greeting, "*Sursum corda, Frater Bernarde, sursum corda* ".[4]

(*c*) In the life of Juniper, there is the conversation as to how to fight the temptations of the flesh.[5]

(*d*) In the life of Haymo of England, we find B. Giles' exclamation on hearing of the fall of Elias : "*Volo descendere quantum possum, quia ille tantus cecidit propter saltum* ".[6]

(*e*) In the life of S. Bonaventure, reference is made to the death of B. Giles as having taken place in 1262.[7]

(*f*) In the life of Conrad of Offida, there occurs the story of Conrad's vision of B. Giles, who breathed into his mouth and conveyed to him the gift of ecstasy.[8]

Reference might be made to other manuscript sources which mention Giles incidentally, such as Nicholas Glassberger, Bartholomew of Pisa, Hubert of Casale, Alvarus Pelagius, but

---

[1] Anal. Franc., iii. p. 4.
[2] *Ibid.*, p. 34.
[3] *Ibid.*, p. 42.
[4] *Ibid.*, p. 44.
[5] *Ibid.*, p. 60.
[6] *Ibid.*, p. 251.
[7] *Ibid.*, p. 328.
[8] *Ibid.*, p. 428.

such references are of quite minor importance and are mostly mere reminiscences or extracts from older and more authoritative sources. Those already enumerated are sufficient to show that only very fragmentary accounts of B. Giles exist in the chief Franciscan documents, apart from the various versions of his life which will now be considered in greater detail.

A large number of MSS. exist containing the Life of B. Giles. They may be divided according to two different systems of classification. One classification is those which contain the Short Life and those which contain the Long Life. The other classification is those which contain the Life by itself and those which contain the Life as part of a cycle. The former appears the more satisfactory classification, as it is based upon the most essential critical question, viz. the authorship of the Life.

Ever since the learned editors of the COLLEGIUM S. BONAVENTURAE of QUARACCHI published in 1897 their edition of the "Chronicle of the XXIV Generals," containing the Long Life, there has been debate concerning the relation between the Long Life and the Short Life. There has been general agreement based on traditional grounds, and especially upon the testimony of Salimbene already quoted, that the author of the original Life of B. Giles was Brother Leo, the disciple and confessor of St. Francis and the intimate friend of B. Giles. It is also generally agreed that the original Life—in the exact form in which Leo wrote it—is not at present extant. It will be referred to in these pages as [L.].

The Short Life, which will be referred to as L 1, is found in seven MSS.

1. CODEX 1/63 in the CONVENT OF THE FRIARS MINOR OF S. ISIDORE, ROME. 12ᵐᵒ, XIV century.

Prol. Hic incipit vita et quaedam verba sancti fratris Ægidii magnae contemplationis, qui fuit quartus in ordine post beatum Franciscum.

Incip. Ad excitandam devotionem nostram.

Explic. Usque modo scripsimus aliqua, (quae) notavit frater sanctus socius beati Francisci. Amodo scribemus aliqua, quae notaverunt socii et familiares ejusdem sancti fratris Ægidii, de multis pauca valde notabilia.

This is the MS. published by Fr. Leonardus Lemmens, O.F.M., in 1901 in "*Documenta Antiqua Franciscana*," *Pars I.* It has not been published anywhere else. Following Lemmens it will be referred to as A.

2. CODEX F. XI 9 in the COMMUNAL LIBRARY OF SIENNA, XIV century, formerly in the suppressed Convento dell' Osservanza of Sienna. A copy of St. Bonaventure's "*Legenda Maior*" of St. Francis occupies fol. 1r-116v. Then follows the Life of B. Giles, fol. 116v-119v.

Rubr. Incipit vita fratris Egidii de ordine fratrum minorum. De innitio (sic) *penitentie, medio et fine.*

Incip. Ad exercendam devotionem nostram.

Explic. gratissimus deo et hominibus fuit de beneficiis sibi collatis. Explicit vita sancti Egidii scripta et compilata per fratrem Leonem socium eius et sancti Francisci. Amen.

This MS. has been described by P. Henricus Bulletti, O.F.M., in "*Archivum Franciscanum Historicum*," *Ann.* viii., *Fasc.* i.-ii. pp. 12-22, in which he has collated it with A.

It will be referred to as S. (for Sienna).

These two MSS., A. and S., are the only ones at present known which contain the Life of B. Giles in a separate form and not as part of a cycle, complete or otherwise.

The remaining five MSS. containing the Short Life belong to the well-known cycle which is frequently described by Franciscan students as the "*Fac secundum exemplar*" collection. It is also known as the "*Legenda Antiqua*" or as the "*Speculum Vitae*". That cycle, the origin and composition of which is still one of the most difficult and obscure questions in Franciscan studies, is an amalgam of a number of older documents.

The collection derives its name "*Fac secundum exemplar*" from the fact that it generally has a sermon upon those words at the beginning. It generally also contains :—

(*a*) A large number of chapters of the *Speculum Perfectionis*.

(*b*) The bulk of the *Actus B. Francisci et Sociorum Ejus*.

(c) The *Testamentum Sancti Francisci*.

(d) The *Admonitiones Sancti Francisci*.

(e) The *Aurea Verba Beati Egidii*.

(f) The Short Life of B. Giles.

The following are then the principal MSS. of this cycle, containing the Short Life :—

3. CODEX VATICANUS 4354. The Short Life is to be found ,in fol. 143a-152a. It contains the four additional chapters, to which reference has been made as forming part of the "*Actus B. Francisci*". This MS. has been very fully and exactly described by M. Paul Sabatier in his "*Speculum Perfectionis*" (Coll. de Documents, etc., Tome i., 1898), pp. clxxvi-clxxxvi. Following Lemmens, it will be referred to as B.

4. CODEX ROYAL LIBRARY, BERLIN, 196 : late XIV or early XV century. The Short Life appears in fol. 66a-85a. This MS. also contains the four additional chapters. It has been described by M. Sabatier in the volume already quoted, pp. clxxxvii-cxcvi.

5. LIEGNITZ CODEX, ARCHIVES OF S. PETER AND S. PAUL (date *circa* 1480). The Short Life is in chapters cxxxix-clii. This MS. is described in "*Opuscules de Critique Historique*," tom. i., p. 31. The Life of B. Giles is there followed by these sentences :—

" *Usque modo scripsimus aliqua quae notavit fr. Leo socius S. Francisci. Amodo scribemus aliqua quae notaverunt socii et familiares ejusdem sancti fratris Ægidii de multis pauca et valde notabilia.*"

6. CODEX CANONICI MISCELL. 525. OXFORD, BODLEIAN LIBRARY (date *circa* 1384). The Short Life is found in fol. 139b-145b. The four additional chapters are again present, but preceding the Life. The text of the Life ends with words closely similar to those in Liegnitz :—

" *Usque modo scripsimus aliqua quae notavit beatus frater Leo socius sancti Francisci. Amodo scribemus aliqua quae notaverunt socii et familiares ejusdem beati fratris Ægidii de multis pauca valde notabilia.*"

7. CODEX CANONICI MISCELL. 528. OXFORD, BODLEIAN

LIBRARY. Last of all we come to the MS. containing the text of the Short Life which forms the basis of the present edition. As this MS. has not been hitherto used in connection with the study of B. Giles, and has not been described except many years ago in the catalogue of Canonici MSS., it appears best to describe it here. It will be referred to as C. (for Canonici).

CANONICI MISC. 528.

A quarto MS. measuring 146 mm. × 105 mm., on paper containing 232 leaves. XV century. The signature of the scribe, Fr. John de Viselbech, appears on fol. 46v. "*Per manus fratris Johannis Viselbech de provincia Saxonie et signanter de conventu Erffordensi*," and on folios 163r, 183r, 192r, 199r, 204v.

Fol. 157v. *Rubr. In nomine domini Incipit Regula et vita minorum fratrum.*

Incip. Honorius episcopus servus servorum dei.

The Rule which follows is that of Honorius as contained in the Bull "*Solet annuere*".

Fol. 163r. *Explicit regula fratrum minorum per fratrem Johannem Viselbech de provincia Saxonie.*

Fol. 163v. *Rubr. Incipit doctrina fratris Egidii layci quondam beati Francisci socii vita eiusdem satis devota.*

Incip. Verba quedam fratris egydii.

This section contains the Golden Sayings of Brother Giles. It breaks off at the foot of 167v and resumes on 205r continuing to 217r. *Explic. beneficia non possunt comprehendi.* It is followed by :—

Fol. 217r. *Rubr. Quomodo frater Egidius venit ad sanctum Franciscum.*

Incip. Ad excitandum (sic) *devotionem nostram.*

Fol. 226r. *Explic. de beneficiis sibi collatis.*

Followed by the following rubricated note :—

Explicit vita beati Egidii quam composuit frater leo et scripsit propria manu deo laus semper anno m.cccc°xxxviii in vigilia Ascensionis.

The remaining pages, 226v-231r, contain religious material

of no special interest and not connected with the Franciscan Order.

The pages intervening between the two sections of the Golden Sayings of Brother Giles, i.e. from fol. 167v-205r, are as follows :—

Fol. 168r-169r. Title. *" Testamentum sancti patris nostri Francisci."*

Incip. Dominus ita dedit mihi.

Explic. istam sanctissimam benedictionem.

Amen. Explicit testamentum sancti patris nostri francisci.

Fol. 169v-170r. Title. *In nomine domini nostri Jhesu Christi.*

Incip. Fac secundum exemplar.

Explic. et gloria in secula seculorum. Amen.

Fol. 170v-171r. Title. *De perfectione paupertatis, scilicet primo qualiter beatus Franciscus declaravit voluntatem super observantiam regulae.*

Incip. Beatus Franciscus tres fecit regulas.

Explic. Et territi decesserunt (sic).

Fol. 171r. Title. *Qualiter beatus f[ranciscus] declarauit intentionem et voluntatem quam habuit a principio vsque ad finem super obseruantiam paupertatis.*

Then follows a rubricated heading :—

De milite volente intrare religionem.

Incip. Legitur de quodam milite.

Explic. devotius obseruaret.

Fol. 171v. *Rubr. Exemplum contra osiositates.*

Fol. 172r. *Incip. Videte quomodo caute ambuletis.*

Fol. 183r. *Explic. in secula seculorum. Amen.*

At the foot of this page the signature of Johannes Viselbech again appears.

The remaining pages up to 205r, where the Golden Sayings resume, contain sundry miscellaneous devotional material of little interest, except for the following points :—

Fol. 184r. This folio ends with the rubricated sentence " Hab got lyp vor alle ding ".

Fol. 186r. The concessions granted to the Brothers Minor

by Eugenius IV at Florence in the year 1435 at the supplication of Nicolas de Ausimo.

Fol. 196r contains a version of the Paternoster in Italian : "Padre nostro che sey in cielo," etc.

Fol. 196v contains a version of the Apostles' Creed in Italian : "Credo in dio padre omnipotente," etc., ending with the rubricated word "Welchz". The same page contains some moral maxims, also in Italian, but apparently in a different but much later hand.

It is difficult to determine with certainty the question whether Johann von Viselbech can be regarded as the scribe of the sections containing the Ægidius material. It is true that the lines at the foot of fol. 226r do not give his name, while they do give a date which is not far distant from the date on fol. 186r which is apparently Johann Viselbech's work. A close examination of the MS. leads to the conclusion that Johann Viselbech's handwriting varied a good deal : that some characteristics, which are found throughout some sections, are absent in others : that for some sections he used a different ink : and, generally, that while it cannot be positively asserted that he was the scribe who wrote the Ægidius pages, there is insufficient evidence for assigning those pages to a different hand.

A comparison of Canonici Misc. 528 with the other MSS. mentioned, viz. 3, 4, 5, 6 above, will show that this MS. is undoubtedly a member, though decidedly a somewhat disjointed member, of the "*Fac secundum exemplar*" cycle. It is interesting to note, however, that it possesses this point of difference from them, that it does *not* contain the four additional chapters. It might even be conjectured that in Can. Misc. 528 we have to deal with the "*Fac secundum exemplar*" cycle in the making, but not yet in the form which it assumed later.

The Long Life of B. Giles has not been discovered up to the present in any MS. in a separate form. It exists solely as a portion of the cycle known as the "Chronicle of the XXIV Generals," a XIV century compilation to which reference has already been made (p. 27). This Chronicle, admirably edited by the COLLEGIUM S. BONAVENTURAE and forming Vol. III.

of *Analecta Franciscana*, contains the Long Life of Blessed Giles in pp. 74-115. The Chronicle, according to the Quaracchi Editors, is found in the following thirteen MSS. : Codex misc. 329, Mun. Lib., Assisi (late XIV cent.) : Cod. 53, Leopold., Med. Laurent. Lib., Florence (XV cent.); Cod. 279, Riccard. Lib., Florence (late XIV or early XV cent.) ; Cod. P. 37 F., Lib. of Conv. S. Maria Angel., Hall (Tyrol) (late XV cent.) ; Cod. I. G. 17, Univ. Lib. Lemberg, Austria (late XV cent.) ; Cod. VIII, C. 7, Nat. Lib., Naples (XV cent.) : Cod. in Lib. of Conv. S. Annunciat. O.F.M., Parma (A.D. 1453): another ditto (XV. cent.) : Cod. 9 L in Lib. of Conv. S. Peter, Rezzato (late XIV or early XV cent.): Cod. lat. 1756, Lib. Angel., Rome (late XIV cent. or early XV) : Cod. in Lib. of Conv. S. Bernardino, Sienna (A.D. 1451): Cod. G. XIV 21, Lib. of Conv. S. Bernardino, Trient (XVII cent.) ; Cod. 3417, Pal. Lib., Vienna (A.D. 1470).

These MSS. do not differ among themselves sufficiently to make it necessary to describe them individually, more especially as a full description is given in the Introduction to *Anal. Franc.*, III. Nor will it be necessary for the present purpose to refer to them separately; the Long Life of B. Giles contained in all of them can be quoted generically as L2.

Summing up then to this point, there are extant seven MSS. containing the Short Life, L1 (two of them by itself in separate form), and thirteen MSS. containing the Long Life, L2.

The main question to be solved is :—

Which of these two Lives is the nearer to the hypothecated original Life written by Brother Leo ?

Or to state the problem in another form :—

Is the Long Life [1] an expansion of the Short Life, or is the Short Life a preçis or abstract of the Long Life ? The present writer, after prolonged examination of the two versions, and after subjecting them to tests of higher and of lower criticism, has come to the conclusion—in agreement with P. Leonardus Lemmens and P. Henricus Bulletti, and in disagree-

---

[1] Not necessarily in the exact form in which it is found in " XXIV Gen.," but perhaps in an earlier form from which the present L2 is derived.

ment with P. van Ortroy and to a lesser extent M. Paul Sabatier, that the Short Life is the earlier, more authentic version,
and the closer to the original work of Leo, and that the Long
Life is an expansion based upon it or upon some cognate form.

The whole trend of the growth of Franciscan documents
or materials is on the lines of accretion rather than of abstrac-
tion. Many instances could be given of the simple original
document finding its way into the more elaborate and complex
later document, e.g. I Celano and II Celano expand with
additions from other sources into Bonaventura's Legend [1] :
the *Speculum Perfectionis* passes into the *Actus B. Francisci*,
and the *Actus* in its turn gets absorbed into the *Speculum Vitae*
in its " *Fac secundum exemplar* " form, which later on evolves
into the *Speculum Vitae* in its printed form. Nor is this process one peculiar to Franciscan documents. It is the characteristic mediæval method. The mediæval author—especially
the chronicler or hagiographer—was generally a compiler : he
habitually used the scissors and paste method.

Consequently, if two Lives of B. Giles exist, one a short
one and the other a much longer one, containing the greater
part of the Short Life, it is antecedently probable that the
Short Life will prove on examination to be the original and
the Long Life the compilation. It would of course be going
too far to deny the possibility of the opposite process—that of
contraction. Such a position would be manifestly untenable,
for Cod. 1/73 in St. Isidore's, Rome, is clearly a mere compendium of L1. It remains, however, true that the whole
problem might not unreasonably be approached with the pre-
supposition that the Long Life is likely to be a compilation,
of which the Short Life is one element.

It has already been pointed out that L1 is found in two
MSS. in a separate, self-contained form, whereas L2 is nowhere
found as a separate entity. From these facts the deduction is

---

[1] It is quite true that in the matter of individual incidents St. Bonaventura
curtails rather than expands his sources, as Goetz points out in his " Quellen zur
Geschichte des hl. Franz von Assis," p. 98, but that does not affect his general
method of absorbing a number of sources into one.

that L1 was originally composed as a separate document, before it came to be incorporated in the "*Fac secundum exemplar*" cycle: but that L2 never existed separately, and first assumed its present form from the pen of the compiler of the "Chronicle of the XXIV Generals". Now it is generally admitted that the "Chronicle of the XXIV Generals" was not completed much before 1374, whereas the "*Fac secundum exemplar*" cycle was in existence by 1328.[1] This points to L1 as much the earlier document.

These arguments may perhaps be discounted as vague generalities. When the actual documents are handled, striking results are obtained.

L2 soon reveals itself as a mere compilation: the two largest elements are (*a*) L1 and (*b*) the Golden Sayings of B. Giles: but in addition the author or compiler can be shown to have drawn upon (*c*) the Legend of the Three Companions. (*d*) The Legend of Andrew of Spello. (*e*) Either I Celano or the *Liber de Laudibus* of Bernard of Bessa.[2] (*f*) The *Vita f. Leonis* in *Speculum Vitae*. (*g*) The *Testamentum S. Francisci*. (*h*) Other unknown sources not at present identified.

The presence of (*a*) and (*b*) can be easily demonstrated by going through L2, underlining the portions which agree verbally or substantially with the two documents in question.

The use of the Legend of the Three Companions will be found on pp. 75-76 in the narrative of the reception of B. Giles: this episode raises several critical problems of special interest. The dependence of L2 upon the Three Companions will be seen by setting out the parallel passages[3] and indicating in capitals the points of verbal similarity:—

XXIV Gen. (L2).	*Three Companions.*
Eodem vero tempore beatus Franciscus, ut novus praeco	Coeperunt[4] POST DUOS ANNOS A SUA CONVERSIONE viri qui-

[1] For evidence in support of this date see J. Joergensen, "St. Francis of Assisi," 1912, p. 393. [2] *Anal. Franc.*, III. p. 666.

[3] In these quotations it appears best to copy the extracts from the printed versions without alterations of spelling, e.g. use of u and v.

[4] Marcellino da Civezza's edition (1899), p. 50.

Regis humilitatis et poenitentiae vias exemplo mirabili praeparans, POST DUOS ANNOS A SUA CONVERSIONE quendam virum mirabilem, prudentia decoratum, multis divitiis redundantem, Bernardum nomine, et quendam alium, Petrum Cathanii nominatum, traxit ad cultum evangelicae paupertatis. Nam sancti Francisci consilio OMNIBUS suis DISTRACTIS et PAUPERIBUS DISTRIBUTIS, poenitentiae et evangelicae perfectionis regulam, assumpto fratrum Minorum HABITU, cum fervore maximo servare statuerunt.

dam exemplo ipsius ad poenitentiam animari.

Abiit[1] itaque dominus Bernardus, qui erat dives valde, et venditis omnibus, quae habebat, multaque pecunia congregata, PAUPERIBUS civitatis DISTRIBUIT universa. . . . DISTRACTIS autem OMNIBUS, HABITUM . . . ambo pariter susceperunt.

The next passage is more striking :—

| *XXIV Gen. (L2.)* | *Three Companions.* |

Quem videns frater Ægidius, prostratus ad terram coram Sancto, HUMILITER GENUFLECTENS se ab ipso IN SOCIETATEM SUAM RECIPI affectuosissime suplicavit. QUEM CUM Sanctus VIDERET FIDELISSIMUM ET DEVOTUM dixit sibi, etc.

Ægidius[2] . . . venit ad eos, et cum magna reverentia et devotione, FLEXIS GENIBUS, rogavit virum Dei, ut eum IN SUA SOCIETATE RECIPERET. QUEM CUM vir Dei VIDERET FIDELISSIMUM ET DEVOTUM, etc.

It is a trifle, worth notice perhaps, that the compiler of L2 finding in Three Companions that Giles on meeting St. Francis falls down before him (*flexis genibus*), reproduces even this detail (*humiliter genuflectens*), which, however, does not appear in L1 or in any other account of the incident.

Of more significance is the following passage, relating to

---

[1] L.c. 54.   [2] L.c. 56.

the giving of the mantle to a poor woman : in position the incident is given by both L1 and L2 immediately after the reception of B. Giles. The Three Companions give an entirely different account of the incident in Chapter XI : their Legend does not attribute the act to B. Giles by name, but to "a certain secular brother " : the whole setting is different, and yet there are certain remarkable similarities of diction between L2 and Three Companions, which do not exist as between L1 and L2.

XXIV Gen. (L2.)	*Three Companions.*
Et STATIM VISUM fuit sibi QUOD ILLA COELUM ASCEND-ERAT, ET SENSIT PROTINUS NOVO GAUDIO SE PERFUNDI.	STATIM [1] . . . VISUM est ei QUOD eleemosyna ILLA in COELUM ASCENDISSET, ET SENSIT NOVO GAUDIO SE PER-FUNDI.

The handiwork of the copyist and compiler is quite manifest in this sentence. The authors of the Three Companions have the figurative idea that the alms ascends into heaven : the compiler of L2 fails to grasp the figure, and says instead that the woman ascended into heaven !

We have next the incident of the journey of St. Francis and B. Giles to the March of Ancona.

XXIV Gen. (L2.)	*Three Companions.*
BEATUS autem FRANCISCUS statim cum FRATRE ÆGIDIO versus MARCHIAM ANCONI-TONAM perrexit. Et SANCTUS VOCE ALTA ET CLARA DECAN-TANS GALLICE per viam Dominum magnifice collaudabat. Tandem DIXIT FRATRI ÆGI-DIO : " SIMILIS ERIT NOSTRA RELIGIO PISCATORI, QUI MIT-TIT RETIA SUA IN AQUAM, CAPIENS MULTITUDINEM PIS-	BEATUS[2] FRANCISCUS, assu-mens FRATREM ÆGIDIUM secum, ivit in MARCHIAM AN-CONITANAM ; . . . vir SANC-TUS, ALTA ET CLARA VOCE laudes Domino GALLICE CAN-TANS, . . . DIXIT autem Sanctus Franciscus ad FRA-TREM ÆGIDIUM " NOSTRA RELIGIO SIMILIS ERIT PISCA-TORI, QUI MITTIT RETIA SUA IN AQUAM, CAPIENS PISCIUM

[1] L.c. 76.   [2] L.c. 58.

CIUM COPIOSAM, ET MAGNOS ELIGIT, PARVOS IN AQUA RE-LINQUENS". Et miratus est frater Ægidius de huiusmodi prophetia videns, parvum adhuc numerum esse fratrum. LICET AUTEM Sanctus adhuc POPULO non PLENE PRAEDI-CARET, TAMEN HORTABATUR per loca viros ac mulieres, UT DEUM diligerent ET TIME-RENT et POENITENTIAM facerent DE PECCATIS. Et FRA-TER ÆGIDIUS, UT sibi CRED-ERENT, cum OPTIME diceret, ADMONEBAT.

MULTITUDINEM COPIOSAM, ET PARVOS IN AQUA RELINQUENS, MAGNOS ELIGIT in vasa sua".

LICET AUTEM vir Dei non-dum PLENE POPULO PRAEDI-CARET, . . . TAMEN . . . HORTABATUR omnes, UT ama-rent ET TIMERENT DEUM at-que POENITENTIAM agerent DE PECCATIS.

FRATER autem ÆGIDIUS ADMONEBAT audientes, UT EI CREDERENT, quia eis OPTIME consulebat.

The historical accuracy of the Three Companions and of the compiler of L2 in the matter of this incident has been severely criticised. For the "Three Companions" alone gives this account of a missionary journey undertaken when St. Francis had three disciples only. Both Thomas of Celano and St. Bonaventura are silent as to such a journey, and both speak of the occasion when the eight set forth, two and two, as the first. Still, the simile as to the fisher has the genuine Franciscan ring about it, and doubtless both the Three Companions in recording it and L2 in copying it are going back to an authentic tradition.[1]

The use of the Legend of Andrew of Spello is found on pp. 100-101, where an incident is attributed to the life of B. Andreas of Burgundy. The Quaracchi Editors say in a footnote: "*Idem refertur de B. Andrea ex Hyspello* († 1254) *de quo vide Breviarium Rom. Seraph. et Acta Sanctorum 3 Junii*".

The *Acta Sanct. 3 Junii,* p. 357, give an account of Andreas of Spello. They quote a statement copied in 1689

---

[1] See also p. 46.

from an earlier document by John de Targurinis, dated 1368, purporting to be a compendium of an earlier work by Thomas Hispellas, Ord. Min., written in 1270. The passage is as follows :—

"*A.D. MCCXLIX. Andreas in conventu Carceris fuit a Bambino Jesu sua praesentia consolatus sed a sonando vespertino perturbatus quoniam eum relinquere opus fuit, eundi gratia ad Vesperas. Et postea, rediens subito Jesus ei dixit: 'Bene fecisti, Andreas, si aliter fecisses, hic me non invenisses. Potes aliquando relinquere Creatorem pro creatura. Sequere, sequere, ego semper tibi propitius ero.'*"

It would appear that the compiler of L2 has confused Andreas of Burgundy with Andreas of Spello and has quoted this story about him, probably from the original work of Thomas of Spello (1270), which is now known only in the *Compendium* of John de Targurinis.

At least one passage in L2 appears to be a quotation or a reminiscence either from the First Life of Thomas of Celano or from the *Liber de Laudibus* of Bernard of Bessa. This is the passage on p. 79, of the distress of B. Giles at being called a hypocrite by a priest. Both Celano and Bernard tell the story of "a certain brother" without specifying B. Giles. On the whole it is more likely that Bernard of Bessa was the source from which the compiler of L2 drew. There is little evidence, if any, that he had ever seen the First Life of Celano, which had of course been suppressed as much as possible before his time.

It is difficult to determine from what source the compiler of L2 derived his story, used in three places in the "XXIV Generals," how Brother Leo consulted B. Giles as to the breaking of the vase in which Elias of Cortona was collecting gifts for the erection of San Francesco. The story is found in a form possessing marked similarities to that of L2 in the *Vita f. Leonis* in the *Speculum Vitae* printed in 1509. It would of course be questionable to assert that L2 drew upon the *Speculum Vitae*, when in view of the relative dates the opposite process might have been the case. But there is good reason to suppose that the *Speculum Vitae* printed in 1509 is based upon very much more primitive documents, probably anterior to L2, and it may quite well be one of L2's sources.

In at least one place, viz. p. 77, of *Anal. Franc.*, III., use has been made of the Will of St. Francis, where it is recorded how B. Giles, if unable to earn a bare living by his labours "recurrebat AD MENSAM DOMINI PETENDO ELEEMOSYNAM OSTIATIM".

But when all these sources have been taken into account, there still remains in L2 a considerable residuum which it has been impossible so far to trace to any particular source. It is possible that some day some fresh source will be discovered from which this unknown material will be derived : but on the whole it is more likely that this residuum constitutes part of the floating oral tradition, which was handed down in connection with the early disciples of St. Francis.

Sufficient has been said, however, to demonstrate that L2 is a mere compilation which yields readily to literary solvents and drops into its constituent elements. The important point to notice is that one element in it, and that the backbone of it, is the document which appears in a separate form and also in the "*Fac secundum exemplar*" cycle, the document which has been quoted as L1. L1 does not drop to bits : L1 cannot be shown to be derived from earlier sources : and why? Because it is a whole, because it is the work of one man who was an author, not a compiler : and if so, why not Brother Leo himself? For this position, other evidence will be produced.

Before leaving this aspect of the matter, reference may be made to one peculiarity of L2, which is not found in L1. There are seven vernacular passages in L2 :—

(1) P. 36. Bo, bo, molto dico e poco fo.
(2) „ Faite, faite e non parlate.
(3) „ Non dicis la, la, sed dicis ca, ca.
(4) P. 92. O becone, che tu sei.
(5) 101. O mi fratello, o bel fratello, o amor fratello, fami un castello, che no abia pietra e ferro. O bel fratello, fami una cittade, che no abia pietra e ligname.

(6) P. 102. Lasciami iacere, se io non salisco in alto, non posso cadere.

(7) P. 110. Chi sei tu, cui io addimando et chi sono io che t'adomando.

It is noteworthy that all these vernacular passages come in sections which have nothing corresponding to them in L1.

From this somewhat detailed examination of the version of B. Giles' Life found in the "Chronicle of the XXIV Generals," it is necessary to revert once again to the Short Life L1 and consider its claims to be the work of Brother Leo, or at any rate to be nearer to his work than any other known version. In doing this, it will be necessary to use some at any rate of the admirable arguments used by Fr. Lemmens in his controversy with Fr. van Ortroy, S.J.[1]

It is first of all to be observed that the Short Life L1 in each MS. claims to be the work of Brother Leo in the most categorical terms.

Codex 1/63 (St. Isidore's, Rome) ends with the following words as to its authorship :—

" *Usque modo scripsimus aliqua quae notavit frater sanctus socius beati Francisci.*"

Codex F XI, 9 (Sienna) is more definite :—

" *Explicit vita sancti Egidii scripta et compilata per fratrem Leonem socium eius et sancti Francisci.*"

The Liegnitz Codex ends thus : —

" *Usque modo scripsimus aliqua quae notavit fr. Leo socius s. Francisci.*"

Codex Canonici Misc. 525 (Oxford) says :—

" *Usque modo scripsimus aliqua quae notavit beatus frater Leo, socius sancti Francisci.*"

Codex Can. Misc. 528 (Oxford) goes even further :—

" *Explicit vita beati Egidii quam composuit frater Leo et scripsit propria manu.*"

---

[1] Lemmens, *Documenta Antiqua Franciscana*, i. (1901), pp. 9-36, answered by van Ortroy in *Analecta Bollandiana*, tom. xxi. pp. 111 *et seq.* : to which Lemmens replies most effectively in *Doc. Antiq. Franc.*, iii. (1902), pp. 8-12.

It is scarcely necessary even to point out with what reserve and caution any such ascription to a mediæval author must be taken. But it is fair to comment that L1 claims Leonine authorship in a way that L2 does not.

Unfortunately we do not possess a single document which can be unhesitatingly accepted as the work of Brother Leo and of him alone. There may be a good deal of his handiwork, probably in a derived form, in the *Speculum Perfectionis*: it is generally admitted that he was one of the traditional "Three Companions," but to what extent we possess their original work either in the document now known as "*Legenda Trium Sociorum*" or in any other form is a problem of great complexity. Nor can Fr. Lemmens' attribution to Leo of the "*Liber de intentione sancti Francisci*" and of the "*Verba S.P. Francisci*," be accepted without reserve,[1] though he has made out a good case. Consequently there is not at present any fixed standard of comparison by which the Leonine authorship of either L1 or L2 can be tested.

The most generally satisfactory test which can be applied is that of historical accuracy, provided that it is not carried too far, or used in too pedantic a spirit. For example, the criticism which has centred around the chapter in L2, describing the visit of St. Louis of France to B. Giles at Perugia, has not always distinguished between historical accuracy and genuineness of tradition. Granted that evidence cannot be produced to show that St. Louis ever was in Italy or ever visited B. Giles at Perugia, that does not of itself prove that the story is not a genuine and integral part of the Legend of B. Giles.

That particular story is full of the unmistakable Franciscan spirit: but the question whether it is historically accurate or not is on quite a different plane from the question whether it can be accepted as part of the original tradition or not.

It is, however, both fair and profitable to apply to the two versions L1 and L2 the test, as to which in matters of fact approaches the more closely to the ascertained results of historical study. The result will be found to be in favour of L1,

---

[1] Lemmens, *Doc. Antiq. Franc.*, Part I. pp. 75-106, Part III. pp. 12-15.

an additional reason for regarding L1 as the nearer to Brother Leo's work. Here are some examples :—

The first relates to the exact place whither B. Giles went to meet St. Francis and join himself to him. The account in L1 is quite clear :—

"*dirigit gressus suos ad ecclesiam Sanctae Mariae de Portiuncula, ubi beatus Franciscus cum dictis duobus fratribus morabatur, quem locum frater Ægidius ignorabat. Cum autem esset in trivio juxta hospitale leprosorum, devote orationi se dedit, ut illuc sine impedimento aliquo Dominus eum dirigere dignaretur.*"

This states definitely three facts : (1) that St. Francis was then living with his first two followers at Sancta Maria de Portiuncula, (2) that B. Giles did not know that spot, (3) that he arrived first at the cross-roads near the Lepers' Hospital.

L2 gives quite a different account :—

"*versus hospitale leprosorum se transtulit, ubi tunc beatus Franciscus in quodam tugurio derelicto cum fratre Bernardo de Quintavalle et fratre Petro Cathanii morabatur.*"

Here the statement is that St. Francis with his two followers was living—not at Sancta Maria—but near the Lepers' Hospital in a tumble-down hut, i.e. at Rivo Torto.

Ingenious attempts have been made to reconcile these divergent statements, which correspond to divergencies in the other early narratives. The most authoritative narrative is that of Thomas of Celano in his First Life : he states clearly (Chapter 21) that those early days were spent at Sancta Maria (*coepit ibidem assiduus commorari*), and that it was after the visit of St. Francis and his eleven followers to Rome for the approval of the Rule, that they took up their abode at Rivo Torto in the abandoned hut. The testimony of St. Bonaventura agrees exactly with this (Chapters II, 8 and IV, 3). So also does the Legend of the Three Companions, which, if it can be taken as accurate, explains the whole matter most clearly. The first home of the Founder and his disciples was Sancta Maria de Portiuncula. Thus in Chapter IX,[1] just before the coming of B. Giles, that Legend says :—

" *Vir autem Dei Franciscus, duobus, ut dictum est, fratribus*

[1] Marcell. da Civ. edn., p. 56.

*sociatus, cum non haberet hospitium, ubi cum eis maneret, simul
cum ipsis ad quamdam pauperculam ecclesiam derelictam se transtulit, quae Sancta Maria de Portiuncula dicebatur. Et fecerunt
ibi unam domunculam, in qua aliquando pariter morarentur.*"

A little further on, in Chapter XI,[1] the brothers, now six
in number, return to Sancta Maria :—

" *Statuto termino, omnes ad Sanctam Mariam de Portiuncula
sunt reversi.*"

Again in the same chapter they are still at the Portiuncula :— [2]

" *Quadam autem die, venit quidam pauper ad ecclesiam
Sanctae Mariae de Portiuncula, apud quam fratres aliquando
morabantur,*"

though it is doubtful whether the incident here recorded is in
its right chronological setting.

Then in Chapter XIV they are found, after the return
from Rome at Rivo Torto :— [3]

" *Conversabatur adhuc Pater cum aliis in quodam loco iuxta
Assisium, qui dicitur Rivus-tortus, ubi erat quoddam tugurium
ab hominibus derelictum, qui locus ita erat arctus, quod ibi sedere
vel quiescere vix valebant.*"

They quit this and go again to Sancta Maria, where they
had formerly been :— [4]

" *Reliquerunt igitur dictum tugurium ad usum pauperum
leprosorum, transferentes se ad Sanctam Mariam de Portiuncula,
iuxta quam in una domuncula fuerant aliquando commorati,
priusquam ipsam ecclesiam obtinerent.*"

All this is perfectly self-consistent and is not in conflict
either with Thomas of Celano or with St. Bonaventura or with
the LI version of the Life of B. Giles.

Against this the only early evidence is that of the *Speculum
Perfectionis*, a much inferior authority, and even that evidence
is none too clear : Chapter 24 says :—

" *In primordio religionis quum fratres manerent apud Rigum
Tortum.*"

The period after the return from Rome could be quite

---

[1] Marcell. da Civ. edn., p. 72.   [2] *Ibid.*, p. 76.
[3] *Ibid.*, p. 90.   [4] *Ibid.*, p. 92.

correctly described as "*in primordio religionis*," for the Order was not recognised and did not officially come into being until the visit to Rome. Be that as it may, L2 in placing the reception of B. Giles at Rivo Torto is almost certainly inaccurate and has little or no support. Further, assuming that Rivo Torto and the deserted hut can be identified with the Lepers' Hospital outside Assisi, the L1 version becomes even clearer. B. Giles directs his steps to Sancta Maria "which place he did not know": he passes Rivo Torto and it is there that he seeks divine guidance as to the way. He assuredly would not have prayed for guidance where to find the Lepers' Hospital: any child in Assisi would have known that: but he might quite well not know where Sancta Maria was.

Another example of the superior historical authority of L1 is in the incident of the missionary journey with St. Francis to the March of Ancona. The argument from silence is admittedly a dangerous one. L1 says nothing about any such journey either immediately after the conversion of B. Giles or indeed at all. Here again L1 is supported by the best and most authoritative sources, Thomas of Celano and St. Bonaventura. The journey to the March of Ancona rests upon the evidence of L2, supported only by the Legend of the Three Companions. It is not impossible that the story has a basis of truth: the fact that Thomas of Celano does not mention it is not conclusive against it: still less the fact that St. Bonaventura does not mention it, for he makes practically no historical statements outside what he borrows from Thomas of Celano. But in the absence of further positive evidence, L1 must on this matter be regarded as superior to L2.

To sum up the whole case for L1 as nearer to the original work of Brother Leo than L2 :—

1. It is antecedently unlikely that L1 is a compendium of L2.

2. L2 can be shown to be a complex work, a compilation from six or seven different sources.

3. L1 is in practically every known MS. attributed to Brother Leo, generally by name.

4. L1 is more accurate in its statement of facts than L2.

Having thus reached the position that the Short Life, described generically as L1, is superior to the Long Life, described as L2, because it is nearer to the original work of Brother Leo, already described as [L], it remains to attempt to represent in diagrammatic or genealogical form the inter-relationship between the various extant texts or groups of texts.

First of all, it becomes certain from an examination of C. (Cod. Canonici 528) and S. (F. XI 9, Sienna) that these two MSS. are very closely related and have a common progenitor. The best example of this is, as frequently occurs in the comparison of MSS., an obvious mistake or blunder common to both. On page 56 C. reads : "*quos beatus franciscus direxit ad diuersas vt monerent populum*". S. reads the same. In both it is necessary to supply from A. the word "*prouincias*" after "*diuersas*" to make sense. Another mistake is on page 58: "*iuit ad sanctum Jacobum & ad sanctum Angelum & ad sanctum Nycolaum de Bari*". Both C. and S. have the words "*ad sanctum Jacobum,*" which are probably a mistaken repetition from the previous paragraph. A. and B. omit those words.

Another example is one where it is uncertain whether A. is right or C. and S. On page 60: "*tunc septimo anno sue conuersionis misit eum ad quoddam heremitorium nomine Fabrione*". C. and S. agree in stating that it was in the seventh year. A. says "*sexto anno*". But in addition to these more striking cases there are scores of minor variants in which C. and S. agree as against A.

One remarkable general feature shared in common by C. and S. is the omission of the rubricated headings to the several chapters. On the whole this points to an early date, or dependence upon an early source. The rubricated headings are probably late.

As might be expected there are a number of cases in which there is agreement betwen C. and S. which is shared also by B., as exemplified by Cod. Vat. 4354.[1] Thus on page 54 : "*et*

---

[1] The present editor has not been able to work this out in detail, as he has not had access to Vat. 4354. He has worked upon the B. variants given by Lemmens in his footnotes.

indueret secum [sic] *sicut frater Bernhardum & sanctum fratrem Petrum, qui fuerunt primi fratres* ". So read B., C., and S. all quite correctly. When B. Giles joined St. Francis there were only two brothers, Bernard and Peter. A. on the other hand is mistaken in adding a third, " *et fratrem Silvestrum* ". Silvester did not join till later. Numerous similar examples of agreement between B., C., and S. can be given : e.g. page 58, addition of the clause " *Habent enim cisternas in ciuitate et extra de longe fontes* " : page 62, " *de nocte* " instead of " *deuote* " : page 68, sentence added, " *Item dixit . . . gratiam sibi datam* ".

On the other hand there are numerous clear indications that A. and L2 are somewhat closely connected. Among such may be mentioned : page 51 in Lemmens : insertion of the whole chapter beginning " *Dixit semel* ": page 82, omission of the sentence " *Nam ego sum . . . violenter* ": page 82, omission of the sentence " *Non est mirum . . . modo* ": page 82, omission of the clause " *iuxta festum sancti Benedicti* ".

Further there are a few signs that L2 is connected with C. and S., but somewhat slightly. The best example is (pp. 78-80) that the whole section " *Moram faciens . . . reprehenderet,*" which is in C. and S. and also in L2, is not in A. or B. This may be interpreted to show that the compiler of L2 had access to the common original of C. and S., as well as to A.

Finally there are certain features peculiar to A. and B. which indicate a connection in source between those two.

The interrelation of the MSS. may be tentatively represented as follows in diagrammatic form, but it must be observed that the diagram does not take into account the extraneous sources of L2 :—

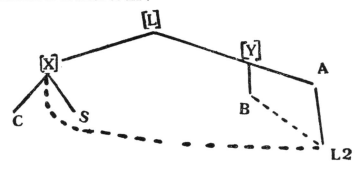

For convenience of reference the MSS. indicated by letters are repeated here, those in [ ] being hypothetical :—

[L] = Original work of Leo.

[X] = Common source of C. and S.

[Y] = Common source of B. and (more remotely) of A.

C = Canonici Misc. 528.

S = Sienna F. XI 9.

B = Vatican 4354. } Collectively L1.

A = S. Isidore's, Rome, 1/63.

L2 = Chronicle of XXIV Generals.

The author wishes, in conclusion, to thank the authorities of the Bodleian Library and Congregation of the University of Oxford for their courtesy in sending the Canonici MS. to the Library of University College, London, for several months for his use ; Professor Robert Priebsch for his advice and help in determining the interrelation of the MSS. ; Mr. Laurence Solomon for his assistance in settling certain difficult readings in the Latin text; and Mr. A. G. Little for his kindness in reading the proofs and making most valuable suggestions upon them.

TEXT OF CANONICI MISC. 528 AND TRANSLATION.

[In editing the Latin text the following principles have been followed :—

Contractions universally recognised are not indicated in the text.

Italics are reserved in order to indicate that the editor is departing from the reading of the MS. Canonici Misc. 528, which is the basis. Where a letter or word is changed, that letter or word is put in italics and the MS. reading given in a footnote : where a letter or word or even a sentence is supplied, it is placed in italics between square brackets.

In order to render the text more easily legible, the capitalisation of the MS. has not been followed : all proper names are spelt with capitals, whether the MS. does so or not : and capitals not required for proper names or for the beginning of sentences are not kept.

For the sake of uniformity, v has been used throughout initially, and u in all other positions.

The Latinity of the text is often peculiar and sometimes bad : obvious mistakes have been corrected, but peculiarities of usage, such as the use of *se* and *sibi*, where the corresponding forms of *is*, *ille* or *ipse* would be expected, have been left.

The sections of the text have been numbered : the numbers used are for convenience of reference the same as those used by Lemmens in his edition in *Documenta Antiqua Franciscana*.]

QUOMODO FRATER EGIDIUS VENIT AD SANCTUM FRANCISCUM.[1]

[Fol. 217 v.] Ad excitandam [2] deuotionem nostram vt feruentius laboremus in opere dei, aliqua verba domini & magna opera eius, que spiritus sanctus est operatus in beatissimo patre nostro Egidio sancto, sicut a sociis suis intellexi & ab eodem patre nostro [3] multoties audiui, ad laudem dei & ad edificationem animarum nostrarum, licet indignus [*scribere curaui*]. Ipse enim met dicebat: "Quanto aliquis plus diligeret bonum alterius, quod dominus operatur in ipso, tanto magis illud bonum efficeretur suum bonum, dum modo sciret illud exfructare & lucrari et custodire, quia bonum non est hominis, sed dei". Item dicebat: "Non sum spiritualis, sicut deberem, & non multum diligo & gaudeo de bono alterius, neque contristor & conpatior de malo & tribulatione alterius, ideo de bono & malo vnde deberem lucrari non lucror, vnde offendo caritatem, *minuitur* [4] bonum & incido in peccatum".

1. Vt autem ab ipso primordio conuersionis sue dominus nobis *ostenderet*,[5] quod nouum & magnum edificium superedificaret in seruo suo, magnam et prerogatiuam gratiam [6] infudit super eum, etiam cum adhuc esset in habitu seculari. Nam cum audisset a quibusdam consanguineis suis & ab aliis, videlicet duobus annis post conuersionem beati Francisci, qualiter Bernhardus sanctus de Quintavalle exemplo et consilio ipsius sancti secundum perfectionem sancti ewangelii vendiderat omnia bona & de consilio beati Francisci distribuerat in

---

[1] Lemmens' version (A.) has an introductory sentence : " Hic incipit vita et quaedam verba sancti fratris Ægidii magnae contemplationis, qui fuit quartus in ordine post beatum Franciscum ". S. reads instead: " Incipit vita fratris Egidii de ordine fratrum minorum. De innitio penitentie, medio et fine." The introductory sentence is probably a later addition to the original text; for a discussion of the phrase " quartus in ordine," see Lemmens, *Doc. Ant. Franc.*, I. pp. 34-35.

[2] MS. "excitandum".   [3] A. adds " auribus meis ".

[4] MS. reads "mittam".   [5] MS. reads " vnde diceret ".

[6] A. reads " magnam praerogativam et gratiam ".

How Brother Giles came to Saint Francis.

To the end that our devotion may be stirred up and that we may labour more zealously in the work of God, I have sought, unworthy though I am, to write down to the praise of God and for the edification of our souls, some words of the Lord and some of His great works, which the Holy Ghost wrought in our most blessed father, Saint[1] Giles, according as I have learned from his companions and have ofttimes heard from the lips of our father himself. For he himself was wont to say : " The more any man cares for the good, which is wrought by the Lord in another, the more does that good bring blessing to himself, if so be that he knows how to husband and increase and tend it, for the good is not of man but of God". Also he used to say : " I am not of spiritual understanding, as I should be, nor do I love much nor rejoice in another's good, nor do I sorrow over and feel compassion for the hurt and suffering of another : and so I profit not from good or ill from which I should profit : wherefore I sin against charity, my good is diminished and I fall into sin."

1. In order that from the very beginning of his conversion the Lord might reveal to us His purpose to build a building new and great in the person of His servant, He outpoured upon him even while he was still in the garb of the world a double measure of His divine grace. For when he had heard from certain his kinsfolk and others, to wit two years after the conversion of Blessed Francis, how that the holy Bernard of Quintavalle,[2] following the example and counsel of the man of God according to the perfection of the holy Gospel, had sold all his goods and by the counsel of Blessed Francis had made distribution thereof in the presence of the Saint himself to many poor folk assembled in the square of Saint

---

[1] It will be observed that the Canonici text generally refers to Giles with the title " Saint," although he has not yet been canonized and although his cultus as Blessed was not confirmed until 1777.

[2] The full story of the conversion of Bernard of Quintavelle is found in I Celano, x. 24, 25, and in the " Chronicle of the XXIV Generals," *Anal. Franc.*, III. pp. 35, 36.

presentia sua pauperibus multis coadunatis in platea sancti
Georgii, vbi nunc est monasterium sancte Clare, statim con-
cepit, qualiter loqueretur cum beato Francisco, vt reciperet
ipsum [Fol. 218 r.] et indueret[1] sicut fratrem Bernhardum
& sanctum fratrem Petrum,[2] qui fuerunt primi fratres post
beatum Franciscum. Et quia velociter currit sermo [*diuinus*]
& spirat sicut placet, sequenti [*mane*] surgens velociter iuit ad
ecclesiam sancti Georgii, cuius solempnitas eo die celebr*aba*-
tur,[3] orans deuote & oblatione facta, apud ecclesiam sancte
Marie de Portiuncula dirigit gressos suos, vbi beatus Franciscus cum duobus suis fratribus morabatur ; quem locum quia
frater Egidius ignorabat, cum esset in triuio iuxta hospitale
leprosorum deuot*e*[4] orationi se dedit, vt illuc dominus sine
impedimento aliquo ipsum dirigere dignaretur ; quem dominus
conduxit ad triuium iuxta locum desideratum, qui ibi sistens
cepit cogitare in desiderio iam concepto. Et quia est dominus prope omnibus inuocantibus eum in veritate & desiderium
pauperum suorum exaudire consueuit, statim venit beatus
Franciscus accedens ad orationem ad siluam,[5] que ibidem
prope erat. Quem videns frater Egidius gauisus est valde,[6]
procidens ad pedes eius : a quo querit sanctus Franciscus quid
vellet. Respondit frater Egidius dicens : "Volo esse vobis-
cum". Cui dixit sanctus Franciscus "Magnum, inquit, fecit
tibi donum [*dominus*]. Esto, inquit, quod Imperator venisset
Assisium & vellet aliquem de ciuitate illa eligere in suum
militem vel camerarium, multi essent, qui hoc affectarent.
Quanto magis debes reputare maius donum, quod de tribu-
lationibus [7] dominus te elegit & vocauit ad curiam suam."
Quem manu propria erigens sanctus Franciscus ad ecclesiam
memoratam duxit, vocauitque sanctum fratrem Bernhardum

---

[1] MS. adds "secum" which is superfluous.

[2] A. adds "et fratrem Silvestrum". B. and S. agree with C. in omitting.

[3] MS. "celebretur".   [4] MS. "devoti".

[5] A. reads "redens ab oratione a silva" thus agreeing with L2, "revertens
de silva, ubi iverat ad orandum".

[6] MS. adds "&" superfluous.

[7] A. B. and S. read "tribus". Lemmens corrects this to "his omnibus".
C. here appears the best text.

George (where now stands the convent of Saint Clare[1]), he bethought him forthwith that he would hold converse with Blessed Francis, and beseech him to receive him and clothe him, as he had done to Brother Bernard and to the holy Brother Peter who were the first brothers after Blessed Francis. And since the word of God runneth swiftly and bloweth where it listeth, he rose betimes on the next day and went in haste to the Church of Saint George, whose feast was that day being observed :[2] there he prayed devoutly, and having been present at the great Sacrifice, he turned his steps towards the Church of Saint Mary of the Portiuncula where Blessed Francis then abode with his two brothers.[3] But since Brother Giles knew not this place, when he was at the cross-roads hard by the Lepers' Hospital, he gave himself devoutly to prayer, that the Lord would be pleased to direct him thither without any hindrance. Then the Lord led him to the cross-roads beside the spot which he sought. And standing there he began to reflect upon the desire which he had conceived. And because the Lord is nigh at hand to those who call upon Him in sincerity and truth and is attentive unto the longing desires of His poor ones, forthwith Blessed Francis drew nigh coming for prayer[4] to the wood which was near by. When he saw him, Brother Giles rejoiced with great joy and cast himself down at his feet. Saint Francis asked of him what he sought, and Brother Giles answered him saying, " I desire to be with you ". To whom answered Saint Francis : " It is a great gift which the Lord hath given thee. Suppose that the Emperor came to Assisi and sought from the city one to be his knight or his chamberlain, many there would be who would earnestly desire this

[1] The Clares were moved in 1260 from San Damiano to the present convent attached to the Church of Saint George.

[2] The Feast of St. George, April 23rd, is now likewise observed as that of B. Giles.

[3] For a discussion of the critical questions arising from this passage, see pp. 44-46.

[4] The various MS. versions leave it uncertain whether St. Francis was coming for prayer to the wood or returning from prayer in the wood.

dicens "Vnum [Fol. 218 v.] bonum fratrem dominus misit nobis". Qui simul in domino gauisi comederunt.

QUOMODO FUIT INDUTUS FRATER EGIDIUS A BEATO FRANCISCO.

2. Et assumens sanctus Franciscus fratrem Egidium accessit ad ciuitatem Assisii, vt tunicam acquireret, vt indueret eum. *Et*[1] cum sic incederent ambo, ecce quedam mulier paupercula valde humiliter et reuerenter petiit elemosinam a beato Francisco amore Christi repetens illud idem; qui cum nichil haberet vnde posset illius inopie implere defectum, non dabat responsum: qu[*ar*]e[2] illa tertio repet*iit*[3] illud idem. Quo[*d*][4] audiens frater Egidius, qui erat cum sancto, adhuc in habitu seculari, non modicum anxius exspectabat vt sibi diceretur quod eleemosinam daret illi, eo quod timore reuerentiali sancto constrictus nichil audebat respondere. Ad quem sanctus angelico vultu conuersus sic ait: "Diuide, inquit, mant*e*llum[5] tuum"; qui gauisus in domino plurimum de sancto mandato [*quod*] exspectabat sollicite, statim extraxit & illud elargitur, libentissime dedit paupercule mulieri. Et statim dato mantello,[5] vt ipse dixit, tanta fuit sancti spiritus consolatione repletus, quod lingua carnea exprimi non valeret. Et in eodem die induit eum beatus Franciscus: postquam indutus fuit, tanto exhilaratus est gaudio, quod tam indumento pauperculo tegeretur, quod lingua & cor exprimere non valebant.

3. Procedente autem tempore completus est septenarius numerus fratrum, quos beatus Franciscus direxit ad diuersas

---

[1] MS. "vt".   [2] MS. "que".
[3] MS. "repetens".   [4] MS. "quo".
[5] MS. "mantallum", "mantallo".

honour. How much greater a gift oughtest thou to count it, that the Lord hath chosen thee and called thee unto His court." Then taking him by the hand and lifting him up Saint Francis led him to the aforesaid Church and calling the holy Brother Bernard said : " The Lord hath sent us a good brother ". And they rejoiced in the Lord and did eat together.

How Brother Giles was Clothed by Blessed Francis.

2. And Saint Francis, taking with him Brother Giles, went unto the town of Assisi, to get a tunic in order that he might clothe him. And as they thus went their way together, behold a certain poor woman very humbly and reverently sought an alms from Blessed Francis for the love of Christ, repeating those same words. And he, inasmuch as he had nought wherewith he could supply her need, answered her not a word. Wherefore she repeated those same words a third time. Hearing this Brother Giles, who was with the Saint, being still in the garb of the world, waited with no small concern to be bidden to give her an alms, but overcome with holy and reverent fear he durst not answer a word. Then the Saint, turning towards him with angelic countenance spake thus: " Part thy mantle in twain ". And he rejoicing exceedingly in the Lord at the holy command which he thus earnestly awaited, forthwith drew off his mantle and most willingly gave it to the poor woman. And immediately, having given the mantle, as he himself said, he was filled with so great comfort of the Holy Spirit, that human tongue fails to express it. And that same day Blessed Francis clothed him : and after that he was clothed, he was filled with so great joy at being clad in so poor a garb, that neither heart nor tongue could utter it.

3. It came to pass in process of time that the number of the brothers became seven. Then Blessed Francis sent them forth to sundry provinces, bidding them exhort the people to give praise to our Creator, Redeemer and Saviour, and to do wholesome penance. Wherefore Saint Giles went out of de-

[*prouincias*]¹ vt monerent populum, qualiter redderent laudes creatori [*vel*] redemptori & saluatori nostro & vt facerent fructuosam penitentiam.   Vnde sanctus Egidius [Fol. 219 r.]² ad sanctum Jacobum in peregrinationem accessit causa deuotionis, in quo itinere penuriam, famem, frigus, sitim et tribulationes perpessus est.   Sed dominus, qui ab initio sue conuersionis ceperat ipsum consolari, semper in omnibus consolabatur.   Fuit autem tunica vna³ contentus ; nam in eodem itinere, cum obuiaret cuidam pauperculo homini, pietate motus caputium exuit de tunica & dedit illi & sic ambulauit xxj diebus sine caputio.

4. Reuersus [*est*] ta*ndem*⁴ [*Assisium*] ; et quia deuotissimus homo erat et catholicus, iuit ad sanctum Jacobum⁵ & ad sanctum Angelum & ad sanctum Nycolaum de Bari.   Vadens sic per mundum docebat⁶ hominibus et mulieribus, vt timerent et amarent creatorem celi & terre et facerent penitentiam de peccatis suis.   Quadam autem die, cum valde fessus de itinere famem pateretur *qui*evit⁷ et dormiuit iuxta viam ; excitatusque a sompno de beneficio dei qui non derelinquit sperantes in se, inuenit dimidium panem ad caput suum et gratias agens deo, cum manducasset, confortatus est.

5. Iuit etiam vltra mare et visitauit terram sanctam. Tunc cum fecisset moram apud ciuitatem Anchonitanam, vt non comederet panem suum otiose, apportabat aquam de fonte a longe, portans magnum⁸ vas in humero suo & ibat per ciuitatem dicens hominibus et mulieribus, vt acciperent aquam et darent sibi panem amore dei.   Habent enim cisternas in ciuitate et extra de longe fontes.⁹   Non enim verecundabatur seruus dei

¹ S. likewise omits " prouincias," a point which indicates almost conclusively some connection between C. and S.

² MS. adds "iuit " which is redundant.

³ A. reads " prima tunica ".   ⁴ MS. reads " tamen ".

⁵ A. and B. omit " ad sanctum Jacobum" (S. James at Compostella) which C. and S. insert probably by mistaken repetition from the previous paragraph.

⁶ A. and B. " hortabatur homines," etc.

⁷ So read A. and B. and apparently S.   But C. reads "iuit ".

⁸ A. omits "magnum ".

⁹ The sentence "Habent . . . fontes" corresponds closely to B. but is omitted in A.   It agrees exactly with S.

votion on a pilgrimage to the shrine of Saint James [1] : and
on this journey he suffered poverty, hunger, cold, thirst, and
tribulations.   But the Lord, who from the very beginning of his
conversion had comforted him, ever granted him consolation
in all things.   He was content with one tunic ; for meeting
on that same journey a certain poor man, moved with love
he took the hood from off his tunic and gave it to him, and so
for one and twenty days he went on foot without hood.

4. He returned to Assisi and, being a man truly devout
and Catholic, he went to the shrine of Saint Michael the Archangel [2] and to that of Saint Nicholas at Bari. [3]   And going
thus about the world, he taught men and women to fear and
love the Creator of heaven and earth and to do penance for
their sins.   Now one day when he was exceeding weary from
his journey and an hungred, he rested and fell asleep by the
wayside ; and awaking from his sleep he found, by the merci-
ful favour of God who never forsakes those whose trust is in
Him, half a loaf beside his head ; and when he had given
thanks to God and had eaten it, he was strengthened.

5. He went also beyond the sea and visited the Holy
Land.   At that time he was delayed in the city of Ancona, [4]
and while there, in order that he might not eat the bread of
idleness, he would carry water from the fountain which was a
great distance away, and bearing a large vessel on his shoulder
go throughout the city bidding men and women receive the
water and give him bread for the love of God.   For they
had cisterns in the city and fountains a great distance out-

---

[1] The shrine in question is that of St. James at Compostella.

[2] A famous shrine on Mount Gargano in Apulia, so called on account of the
appearance of St. Michael the Archangel to St. Laurence about A.D. 492.

[3] Another famous shrine in Apulia, celebrated for possessing the body of St.
Nicholas which was transported thither in A.D. 1087 and was the cause of many
notable miracles.

[4] The MSS. leave it uncertain whether Ancona is the town meant.   Some
MSS., especially those of the L2 group, read " Achon," referring to S. Jean
d'Acre in Syria.

excelsi humiliare & inclinare se ad omne opus seruile & honestum
propter bonum exemplum, vt de labore manuum suarum panem
comederet.   Nam cum quodam tempore ipse visitaret [Fol. 219
v.] dominum Nycolaum cardinalem & episcopum tusculanensem,
et ibat ad iuuandum ipse homines ad colligendum oliuas &
alia seruitia, & accipiebat panem pro labore suo & sic apportabat ad domum cardinalis.   Et cum diceret sibi cardinalis
vt tamquam pauper manducaret de pane suo, ipse *ei* dicebat [1]
verbum propheticum : " Labores manuum tuarum manducabis
etc.".   Sicut et beatus Franciscus docuit primo fratres suos &
in regula fecit scribi et in testamento suo prope mortem con-
firmauit.   Quantum laborem, famem, sitim, frigus, inopiam, &
tribulationes et verecundias sustinuit cum gratiarum actione,
sicut ipsemet retulit, longum esset enarrare.

   6. Reuertente [2] autem eo tempore de peregrinationibus suis,
considerans beatus Franciscus per spiritum sanctum quod
Egidius esset homo dei et boni exempli, gauisus valde est
dixitque ei, vt pergeret quo vellet.   Cui sanctus Egidius respondit, quod in tam libera obedientia ire et viuere nolebat.
Tunc septimo [3] anno sue conuersionis misit eum ad quoddam
heremitorium nomine Fabrione in planitie Perusii.
   Et cum respiceret dominus ad ipsum et ad multa opera eius,
facta est super eum manus domini.   Vbi [4] inter alia, que sibi
dominus contulit beneficia sua, cum quadam nocte esset in
oratione, tanta fuit diuina consolatione repletus, quod visum
fuit ei vt dominus vellet educere animam extra corpus, vt lucide
videret de secretis suis et vt magis animaret ipsum ad bene
operandum [5] in seruitio dei.   Et sic incepit sentire a pedibus,

---

   [1] A. " et ipse ei dicebat "; S. " ipse dixit ei " : MS. " ipse enim dicebat ".
   [2] A. reads " Reuertente autem eo de peregrinationibus suis ad sanctum
Franciscum considerans idem sanctus, quod esset homo dei," etc.   S. agrees
with C.
      [3] A. " sexto "; S. " septimo ".   [4] A. " Et "; S. " Ut ".
      [5] A. adds " et roborandum ".

side. For this servant of the Most High was not ashamed to humble himself and lower himself to every menial but honest work as a good example, so that he might eat bread by the labour of his own hands.

Now it came to pass once that he was visiting the Lord Cardinal Nicholas,[1] Bishop of Tusculum ; and he used to go and help men collecting olives and doing other menial tasks, and thus he earned bread by his labours and brought it back to the Cardinal's house. And when the Cardinal told him that as a poor man he should eat of his bread, he answered him in the words of the Prophet: "Thou shalt eat of the labours of thy hands".[2] For even thus did Blessed Francis in the beginning teach the brothers and caused it to be written in the rule[3] and confirmed it in his Testament[4] shortly before his death. Time would fail to tell all things concerning the great toil and hunger and thirst and cold and want and tribulation and shame which he endured with giving of thanks, as he himself recorded.

6. Now when he returned at that time from his journeyings, Blessed Francis, perceiving by the Holy Spirit that Giles was a man of God and a good ensample to others, rejoiced exceedingly and bade him go wheresoever he desired. But Saint Giles answered that he sought not to go or to live in such free obedience. So in the seventh year from his conversion Saint Francis sent him to a certain hermitage named Fabrione in the plain of Perugia.

And when the Lord had regard unto him and to the multitude of his good works, His hand was upon him. There it was that—among other signal favours which the Lord conferred upon him—when he was one night at prayer, he was

[1] The Quaracchi Fathers identify this Cardinal as Nicholas of Clairvaux, generally known as " the Monk " who died in 1227 or 1228. It is known that the Papal Court was at Rieti in 1225, to which date this incident may probably be assigned.

[2] A reference to Psalm cxxviii. verse 2.

[3] In the Rule, Chapter V. " *De modo laborandi* ".

[4] In his Testament, St. Francis says : " *Et ego manibus meis laborabam et volo laborare ; et omnes alii fratres firmiter volo quod laborent de laboritio* ".

qualiter moriebatur corpus, donec anima exiret. Et stans anima extra corpus, sicut placuit creatori nostro, qui ipsam misit in corpore, pre nimia [Fol. 220 r.] pulchritudine sua, qua decorauerat eam spiritus, delectabatur respicere semetipsam. Erat enim subtilissima & lucidissima super existimationam,[1] sicut retulit prope mortem suam. Tunc rapta est illa sanctissima anima contemplando secreta celestia, que nulli reuelauit, vnde dixit: "Beatus homo qui scit[2] conseruare secreta dei, quia [*nihil*] occultum, quod non reueletur, sicut dominus volue*r*it[3] & quando ei placuerit. Timeo enim de me metipso, et ideo, inquit, si sint reuelanda, magis volo, quod reuelentur per alium quam per me."

7. Et quia inimicus humani generis semper nititur molestare sanctos & perfectos viros[4] ex permissione [*dei*], non multo post dictam consolationem in eodem heremitorio suo accidit post orationes suas deuote[5] factas, cum intrasset cellam, sensit post se angelum Sathane, cuius timorem horribile[*m*] non valens sustinere, procidit in oratione & corde supplicans, quia loqui non poterat, deo, statim extitit liberatus. Post dies autem paucos interrogauit beatum Franciscum dicens: "Pater, inquit, est aliquid ita terribile, quod non possit sustineri donec dicatur vnum PATER NOSTER". Respondit beatus Franciscus dicens "Dyabolum non posset quis sustinere, donec diceretur dimidium PATER NOSTER, quin statim moreretur, nisi diuinum adiutorium succurreret". Quo audito sanct*us*[6] Egydi*us*, sicut expertus fuerat, credidit verum esse.

---

[1] A. "aestimationem".   [2] A. adds "custodire et".
[3] MS. "voluit"; A. "voluerit".
[4] MS. adds "et" which is better omitted.
[5] A. "de nocte"; B. and S. agree with C. in reading "deuote".
[6] MS. "sancto Egydio"; A. "beatus frater Egidius".

filled with so great and heavenly a consolation that it seemed to him as if the Lord sought to draw his soul from out of his body, to the end that he might perceive clearly the Divine secrets and might be inspired to labour more zealously in the service of God. And so he began to feel from his feet upwards as if his body were dying, until his soul passed out of his body. And as it pleased our Creator Who placed the soul in the body, the soul standing outside the body gazed with delight upon itself by reason of the exceeding great beauty with which the Spirit had adorned it. For the soul was most subtle and resplendent beyond all conception, as he did tell at the time of his death. Then was that most holy soul caught away by reason of contemplation of the heavenly secrets, which he never revealed to any man, for he said : " Blessed is the man who knows how to keep the secrets of God, for there is nothing hid which shall not be revealed, as the Lord Himself willeth and whensoever it pleaseth Him. But I fear for myself, and thus, if things are to be revealed, I desire that they may be revealed through another rather than through me."

7. And because the enemy of the human race ever strives by the permission of God to trouble those who are holy and perfect, it came to pass that not long after the aforesaid con-solation in the same hermitage, when having devoutly said his prayers he had entered his cell, he felt behind him the angel of darkness. And being unable to bear the fear and horror thereof, he fell to prayer, and, beseeching God in his heart, since he was unable to utter a word, was immediately set free. A few days afterwards he asked Blessed Francis, saying : " My father, is there aught so terrible that it cannot be borne for the time it would take to say one Paternoster ? " Blessed Francis answered saying : " One could not endure the Devil even while one said half a Paternoster, but one would die forth-with, except one were succoured by divine aid ". Having heard this Saint Giles believed it to be true, since he had himself experienced it. Another time in the year when he was at Spoleto in a certain church of Saint Apollinaris where at that time the brothers dwelt, he rose in the night and went

Alio autem tempore, anno hoc cum esset apud Spoletum in quadam ecclesia sancti Apollinaris, [*vbi tunc temporis hospitabantur fratres* [1]] de *nocte* [2] surgens cum [3] intrasset ecclesiam tempestiue, dum inclinatus staret in oratione, sensit super se demonem ipsum nimium opprimentem & molestantem; ipse autem vehementius orans non poterat [Fol. 220 v.] surgere, sed subtraxit se sicut potuit vsque ad vas aque benedicte, qua fide aspersus statim a molestia demonis fuit deliberatus.

8. Anno decimo octauo sue conversionis, quo scilicet beatus Franciscus de hoc mundo [4] migrauit ad celum, cum accederet sanctus [5] Egidius cum socio ad heremum de Scetona [6] quod est in episcopatu Clusino, peruenit ad locum fratrum de Cibostulo, vbi nocte sequenti vidit in sompnis imperatorem *qui* nimia[m] familiaritate[m]ostendebat eidem, quod, ipse dixit, venture [7] glorie signum fuit. Tunc surrexerunt [8] & ad predictum locum accesserunt, ibique quadragesimam sancti Martini feruenter & deuote fecerunt. Vbi sanctus Egidius vidit in sompnis beatum Franciscum, dicens ei: "Vellem, inquit, loqui inter te et me". Ad quem sanctus Franciscus ait: "Stude tibi, inquit, si vis loqui mecum". Cum ibidem oratione & deuotione maxima laboraret, tribus diebus ante natiuitatem domini in nocte cum deuote oraret, apparuit sibi dominus Jesus Christus visibiliter [9] oculis corporeis. In qua apparitione frater Egidius pre nimio odore voces emittebat immensas eique [10] videbatur humanitate deficere, quia talia non poterat sustinere, magnumque fratribus de loco immittebat timorem suis vocibus: subitoque repletus est odore ineffabili & dulcedine cordis immensa; & sic quasi in extremis positus videbatur laborare. Quod autem audiens non modicum incepit quidam frater timere et accedens ad socium

---

[1] Supplied from A. and S.   [2] So A; C. reads "deuote".
[3] A. "cum intrasset ecclesiam et inclinatus staret," etc.
[4] A. "saeculo".
[5] C. and S. read throughout "sanctus E.," where A. gives "beatus frater".
[6] A "septone".   [7] A. "futurae".
[8] A. adds "ipse et socius".
[9] A. adds "eum uidens," which spoils the sense.
[10] A. "et quasi" for "eique".

at the fitting season into the church: and while he stood bowed in prayer, he felt the devil over him, oppressing him and attacking him sore. But though he prayed more earnestly, he could not rise, but dragged himself as best he could to the stoup of holy water ; and having sprinkled himself therewith he was at once set free from the assaults of the Evil One.

8. In the eighteenth year of his conversion, being the year in which Blessed Francis departed from this world to heaven, Saint Giles went with a companion to the hermitage of Cetona[1] in the diocese of Chiusi, and came to a house of the brethren at Cibottola. And there the following night in his dreams he beheld the Emperor who showed exceeding great favour to him, which thing, as he himself said, was a symbol of coming glory. Then they arose and made their way to the aforesaid house and spent the Lent of Saint Martin there in a spirit of fervour and devotion. And there Saint Giles saw in his sleep Blessed Francis and said unto him : " I would speak with thee ". And Saint Francis answered him saying : " Have regard to thyself, if thou wouldest speak with me ". When he had laboured there in prayer and most earnest devotion, three days before Our Lord's Nativity as he was praying devoutly in the night, Our Lord Jesus Christ appeared manifestly before him visible to his mortal eyes, and by reason of this vision and of the inexpressible sweetness of odour Brother Giles uttered great cries thinking himself to be verily at the point of death, for he could not bear such wondrous things ; and great fear came upon the brothers in the house by reason of his cries ; and suddenly he was filled with an unspeakable odour and an exceeding great inward sweetness, and thus he seemed to be indeed at death's door. A certain brother hearing this began to be greatly afraid, and going to the companion of Brother Giles said to him : " Come to Brother Giles, for he is dying ! " And his

[1] The MSS. vary greatly in their rendering of this name. It is Cetona in Tuscany, near Chiusi.

fratris Egidii dixit ei : "Veni ad fratrem Egidium, quia mori-
tur ". Qui continuo surrexit [1] & dixit sancto Egidio "Quid
habes ? " Et ille respondit : " Veni, fili, quia desiderabam te
modo [Fol. 221 r.] videre"; diligebat enim eum valde et de
ipso multum confidebat, quia nutriebat eum ab adolescentia
in sanctis moribus et actibus spiritualibus. Ipse vero qualiter
sibi acciderat [2] enarrauit per ordinem ; socius eius [3] hoc audiens
visionem diuinam esse cognouit & ad cellam suam reuersus est.

9. Sequenti [4] die iuit ad cellam sancti Egidii socius ipsius
et inueniens eum flentem et lamentantem monebat eum,[5] ne
se tantum affligeret, quia possit exinde corpus deficere. Cui
ille respondit : " Quomodo, inquit, non possum flere, cum
inimicum dei me esse cognoscam, et ipse fecit tantam misericordiam mihi & dedit mihi tale donum, quare dubito ne
secundum voluntatem suam in eo [6] operer". Hoc autem
dicebat [sentiens [7]] specialem gratiam sibi datam a deo, in qua
gratia mirabiliter inmutatum et [in]nouatum se sentiens dixit
socio suo : " Vsque modo ibam quo volebam, & que volebam
facere, faciebam laborans manibus meis ; nunc & deinceps non
ita, sicut consueui, facere possum, sed sicut sentio in me,
ita opportet me facere. Super quo valde timeo, ne aliqui
querant [8] de me quod eis dare non possum." Cui socius eius
dixit : " Dominus, qui dat seruo suo gratiam, ipse gratie
largietur custodiam ; tamen bonum est esse timorem dei apud
te". Que responsio placuit ei. Fuit autem in tanta ac tali
dulcedine indicibili & iubilo tam suaui & odore dei tribus diebus
ante natiuitatem domini vsque ad Epyphaniam, non tamen
continue sed interpellatim [9] die et nocte ; non enim poterat

---

[1] A. "surgens venit ad eum dicens : Quid, pater, habes ? "
[2] MS. "acciderit".   [3] A. "ipse autem " for "socius eius ".
[4] A. "sequenti vero die reversus ad cellam ejusdem fratris Egidii". Cf. the
version of this paragraph in L2 (p. 97), which begins "Sequenti vero die ivit ad
cellam fratris Ægidii idem socius," etc.
[5] MS. adds " ut " which is superfluous.
[6] MS. adds "non" superfluously.
[7] Supplied from S. ; A. gives " propter ".
[8] A. adds " a me," with which L2 agrees.
[9] So C. and S. ; but A. "interpolate": B. "interpellate in ": L2 "interpau-
late ".

companion arose forthwith and said to Saint Giles: "What aileth thee?" And he answered: "Come hither, my son, for I was verily longing to see thee"; for he loved him exceedingly and had great trust in him, for he had brought him up from his youth in holy ways and in spiritual deeds. Then the man of God told him in order what things had befallen him, and his companion hearing this perceived that he had had a heavenly vision and returned to his own cell.

9. On the following day Saint Giles' companion went to his cell and found him weeping and lamenting and bade him not afflict himself so sore, since he would thereby do hurt to his body. But he answered: "How should I not weep, when I know myself to be an enemy of God and when He Himself has had such mercy upon me and granted me so great a gift, wherefore I doubt lest what I do is contrary unto His will?" This he said, perceiving that special grace had been given to him of God, by which grace he felt himself marvellously changed and renewed, and he said to his companion: "Until now I walked whither I would and did what I would, labouring with my hands: but now and from henceforth I cannot do as I have been wont, but it behoves me to do as the spirit within moves me. Wherefore I fear greatly, lest some should seek of me what I cannot give them." And his companion answered him saying: "The Lord, who giveth grace to His servant, will Himself watch over that grace; nevertheless it is good that the fear of God is with thee". And this answer pleased him. He continued for the three days before Our Lord's Nativity and from then until the Epiphany in this unspeakable sweetness and in this exquisite joy and divine odour, yet not continuously but at intervals by day and by night: for his mortal nature could not bear it, when the dazzling brightness appeared. He prayed instantly to the Lord, that He should not lay upon him so great a burden, pleading earnestly that he was not fitted therefor, since he was an unlearned and ignorant man, and a simple peasant: but the more he made himself out to be unworthy, so much the more did the Lord

sustinere humanitas, cum apparebat immensa claritas. Ora-
batque ad dominum instanter, vt sibi non imponeret tantum
onus [1] & allegabat multum, quod non erat ad hoc aptus, pro
eo quod erat homo ydeota et sine litteris [Fol. 221 v.] et rusticus
simplex ; quanto autem plus reputabat se indignum, tanto plus
dominus suam gratiam [2] augmentabat.   Dixitque [3] quod in
fine sicut insufflauit in apostolos, ita insufflauit in eum.
Quadam vero nocte stante sancto Egidio [*cum socio*] ante
cellam & dum de verbis domini loquerentur suauiter & deuote,
venit splendor quidam transiens plane inter ambos ; cumque
socius eius ab eo, quid esset, quereret, respondit " Dimitte ire ".
Erat ibi vnus quidam religiosus, cui dominus reuelauerat de
secretis suis.   Nam paulo antequam hoc eueniret sancto
Egidio, viderat in sompnis quod vbi cella sancti Egidii con-
structa erat, ibi sol oriebatur & ad occasum uergebat; qui
postea videns sanctum Egidium mutatione dextre excelsi
mirabiliter immutatum nouo [4] spiritu gratie dixit ei :   " Porta
suauiter filium virginis."

10. Postmodum sanctus Egidius studuit omni qua poterat
sollicitudine custodire [5] gratiam a domino datam sibi ; dicebat
enim : " super omnes [*gratias*] & virtutes [6] hec summa virtus est,
sequi virtutes & custodire gratiam sibi datam".   Item dixit :
" Apostoli postquam receperunt donum spiritus sancti, centies
et millies plus portauerunt maius pondus ad sustinendas
tribulationes et ad custodiendam gratiam sibi datam ".[7]   Ex
tunc fuit & erat semper in cella solitarius, vigilans, orans,
ieiunans et ab omni opere & sermone malo se custodire sollicitus.   Et si quando aliquis vellet ei referre [8] de alio qu*id*piam [9]

[1] A. "tantum et tale onus odoris et dulcedinis": S. "tantum honus
odoris " : L2 "tantum onus ".
[2] A. and L2 add " in eo".
[3] A. " In fine tamen hujus odoris et dulcedinis, dixit : Sicut Deus insufflavit in Apostolos, insufflavit et in me ".
[4] MS. adds "que ".   [5] A. "servare".
[6] A. reads "super omnem gratiam et virtutem esse scire custodire gratiam
a Domino sibi datam ". B. agrees substantially with C. ; S. is practically identical
with C.
[7] A. omits " Item dixit . . . datam " ; B. and S. agree with C.
[8] A. "Si quando autem aliquis voluit beato fratri Ægidio referre ".
[9] MS. "quempiam ".

multiply His grace given unto him.   He said that in the end, just as He breathed upon the apostles, so also He breathed upon him.   Now it came to pass on a certain night, as Saint Giles stood with his companion before his cell and as they held sweet commune together devoutly on things of God, that a certain bright light seemed to pass right between them : and when his companion asked him the meaning thereof, he answered: "Let it be!"   There was a certain Religious there, to whom the Lord had revealed of His secrets.   For a short while before this befell Saint Giles, he had seen in his dreams that where the cell of Saint Giles was builded, there the sun rose and there went also to rest : and afterwards, seeing Saint Giles marvellously transfigured by the hand of the Most High and filled with a new spirit of grace, he said unto him, " Carry tenderly the Virgin's Son ".[1]

10. After this Saint Giles strove with all his might to guard the grace given unto him of the Lord : for he would say that this was the greatest virtue above all other graces and virtues, to follow virtue and to guard the grace given unto him.   He said also : "After that the Apostles received the gift of the Holy Ghost, they had a hundred, yea a thousand times weightier burden to bear, to endure tribulations and to guard the grace given to them ".   From that time he was wont to be always alone in his cell, watching unto prayer with fasting and carefully keeping himself from every evil work or word.   And if anyone at any time sought to tell him aught ill concerning another, he would say thus : " I seek not to know of the sin of another ". And he would say to him who would tell him : " Beware, brother, lest thou see anything which is not for thy good ".

[1] The meaning of this passage is obscure.   It probably means that the Religious beheld Blessed Giles with the Infant Christ in his arms.

mali, dicebat hoc verbum : "Nolo, inquit, scire peccatum
alterius ". Et dicebat referenti : " Caue, frater, ne videas
aliquid contrarium, nisi vsque ad bonum tuum ".[1]

11. Hunc igitur [Fol. 222 r.] seruum bonum et in modico
sibi re*peri*ens [2] dominus fidelem digne[3] sibi maiora commisit ;
cui sibi in tantam sibi gratiam datam augmentauit, [*quod
hominibus non poterat amplius occultari*].[4] Nam si quis cum
eo tractaret de gloria domini eiusque dulcedine siue de paradiso,
statim rapiebatur nec etiam se mouebat de loco. Proinde
subtraxit se non solum a familiaritate secularium, sed etiam a
fratribus suis et aliis religiosis. Dicebat enim : " Securius est
homini, saluare animam suam cum paucis quam cum multis :
hoc est esse solitarius, videlicet vacare deo et anime sue. Quia
solus deus, qui creauit animam, est amicus eius & non alius." [5]
" O quam spirituale donum et prerogatiua gratia,[6] cui datum
est agnoscere [7] anim*am*.[8] Solus deus agnoscit [7] & cui voluerit
reuelare ; " & ideo de se ipso dicebat : "Si sanctus Petrus &
beatus [9] Paulus descenderent de celo & dicerent mihi vt satis-
facerem personis volentibus mihi loqui, non crederem eis ".
Item dicebat : " Qui melius facit factum [10] anime sue, melius
facit factum [10] animarum amicorum suorum". Et iterum :
"Multas consolationes & uisitationes domini potest homo
amittere culpa sua, quod in perpetuum non rehaberet eas ".[11]
Vnde exemplum ponebat de illis, qui ludunt ad taxillo[s],
qui[a] pro vno puncto taxillorum, quod est ita paruum, amittit
homo quandoque multa [12] : sic pro leui peccato, si nesci*erit* [13]
custodire, perdit homo magnum lucrum anime sue. Item
dicebat beatus Franciscus. " Vide, scriptum est ; Caue ne

---

[1] A. " non ad utilitatem tuam ".   [2] MS. " recipiens ".
[3] MS. " dignum ".   [4] Supplied from A.
[5] In this passage " securius . . . alius " C. agrees almost identically with A. ;
but S. reads " Securius est esse solitarius videlicet vacare domino et anime sue
quia deus qui creauit . . . alius ".
[6] MS. " prerogatiuam gratiam " (sic !) ; A. omits.
[7] A. " cognoscere, cognoscit ".   [8] MS. " anime ".
[9] So C. and S. while A. " sanctus ". The fact that C. and S. both read *sanctus*
Petrus et *beatus* Paulus " shows close connection.
[10] So C., with which L2 agrees : but A. reads " faciem ".
[11] A. " quas in perpetuum non recuperabit ".
[12] MS. corrupt here.   [13] MS. " nesciret ".

11. The Lord therefore, finding him a good and faithful servant unto Himself in a very little, committed greater things to him, for which he was counted worthy : and He multiplied so greatly the grace given unto him, that he could no longer hide it from men. For if any man conversed with him concerning the glory of the Lord and His sweetness or concerning Paradise, immediately he fell into an ecstasy and moved not from the spot. And for this cause he withdrew himself not only from converse with those in the world, but also from his own brethren and other religious. For he used to say : "It is safer for a man to save his soul with few rather than with many ; this is to be a true hermit, to be at leisure to yield oneself to God and one's own soul. For God alone, who created the soul, is the soul's friend and not another. O how heavenly a gift and what surpassing grace is his, to whom it is given to know his own soul ! It is God alone who knows the soul and he to whom God is pleased to reveal it." And thus he would say concerning himself : "If Saint Peter and Saint Paul were to descend from Heaven and bid me satisfy the desire of those who wish me to talk, I would not believe them". And also he would say : "He who does good unto his own soul, does good likewise unto the souls of his friends". And again, "A man may of his own fault lose many divine consolations and visitations, in such wise that he may never recover them for ever". He would draw an ensample from those who play at dice, for through one point of the dice which is so small, a man may at times lose much : so by reason of a small sin, if he knows not how to guard himself, a man may lose the great treasure of his own soul. Blessed Francis also used to say : "Behold, it is written, Beware lest thou lose by laughing what thou hast gained by mourning". And therefore Saint Giles from the beginning of his conversion gave himself no rest from being ever at liberty for the Lord and his own soul : and he found favour before the Lord and was counted

ridendo amittas, quod plangendo lucratus es." Et ideo sanctus
Egydius a principio conuersionis sue requiem non dedit
temporibus suis vacare semper domino[1] & anime sue :
inuenit gratiam coram domino & ab ipso meruit honorari, vt
videtur de secretis celestibus, que a tempore beati Francisci
paucis [Fol. 222 v.] fuisse data putamus. Sicut[2] enim quibusdam fratribus retulit, vnde dicebat : " Cum magno timore & cautela oportet custodire secreta dei & thesaurum ".[3]

13. Commenda[ba]t beatus Egidius locum de Ceptone
propter misericordiam dei & gratiam prerogatiuam,[4] quam
ostendit ei in predicto loco super omnia citramarina loca &
vltramarina, sex locis vltramarinis exceptis, quibus etiam hunc
locum comparabat, & dicebat, quod ad hunc locum deberent
homines accedere cum maiore reuerentia & deuotione quam
ad sanctum Angelum vel ad sanctum Petrum vel ad sanctum
Nycolaum vel ad aliquem locum citramarinum, sicut maior
est[5] dominus quam seruus, et sic est Christus maior quam
alii sancti ; dicebatque quod similis huic esse poterat, maior
esse non poterat ; cumque talia diceret, respondit socius suus
dicens sibi : " Pater, inquit, magnum fuit, quod accidit[6]
Aluerne beato Francisco de Seraphim : nobilis etiam virgo
sancta Christina, nobilis etiam sancta Katherina[7] & multe alie

---

[1] A. " sed vacabat Deo " ; B. agrees with C.

[2] The passage " Sicut . . . thesaurum " is contained in C., S., and B., but
not in A.

[3] C. and S. agree in continuing at this point with the paragraph beginning
" Commendabat sanctus Egidius ". A. inserts immediately after the words
" fuisse data putamus " a chapter (Lemmens No. 12) beginning " Dixit semel
frater Ægidius " and ending " qui est benedictus in saecula ". This chapter
corresponds in the main to the chapter " De quodam raptu mirabili coram
domina Jacoba de Septemsoliis," in L2, Anal. Franc. III. 102-104. B. after the
words " et thesaurum suum " proceeds, " Explicit de S. fratre Ægidio," and
then inserts the four chapters which are also given in L2 : " (1) Quomodo
domina Jacoba de Septemsoliis visitavit fratrem Ægidium. (2) qualiter frater
Ægidius extraxit dubium a quodam magistro Praedicatore. (3) quomodo fr.
Jacobus de Massa petivit a fratre Ægidio, qualiter se haberet in raptu. (4) de
revelatione facta in cordibus sancti Ægidii et sancti Ludovici regis."

[4] A. " gratiam et magnam praerogativam ". In three places C. and S. vary
from A. in using " praerogatiuam " as an adjective.

[5] A. " cum sit maior ".   [6] A. adds " in monte ".

[7] B. " nobilis etiam fuit virgo beata Christina et sancta Catharina," with
which L2 agrees, but A. is corrupt at this point and reads " Nobilis etiam
virgo fuit sancta Christiana Katharina ".

worthy to be honoured by God, so that he perceived heavenly
secrets such as we believe to have been revealed to but few
since the days of Blessed Francis. For this he told to certain
of the brethren saying: "With great fear and care should a
man guard the secrets and the treasure of God".

13. Blessed Giles used to praise the place of Cetona because
of the mercy and surpassing grace which God showed unto him
in the said place, above all other places on this side of the seas
and beyond the seas, save only six places beyond the seas
to which also he was wont to compare this place ; for he said
that men should come unto this place with greater reverence,
and devotion than to the shrine of Saint Michael the Archangel
or Saint Peter's or the shrine of Saint Nicholas at Bari or any
other place on this side of the sea, since as the lord is greater
than the servant, so Christ is greater than the Saints. And
he used to say that like unto this a place might be, but greater
it could not be. And when he spake thus, his companion
answered saying unto him : " Father, 'twas a great thing which
befell Blessed Francis on Alverna concerning the Seraphim : a
noble virgin also was Saint Christina, noble also were Saint
Katherine and many other virgins and saints throughout the
world ". To which Saint Giles answered : " My son, the
creature is nought beside the Creator ".

virgines & sancti per prouincias ". Ad hoc sanctus Egidius dixit : " Fili, inquit, non est aliqua creatura in comparatione creatoris ".

14. Alia vice [*erat*] frater Gratianus, eius socius, & frater Jacobus & frater Andreas de Burgundia cum sancto Egidio. Dixit frater Gratianus fratri Andree predicto : " Inuenitur in sacra scriptura, quod dominus noster[1] apparuerit alicui citra mare post resurrectionem suam ? " Hoc autem dixit volens scire veritatem, si aliquid ad hoc responderet Frater Egidius. Respondit sanctus Egidius cum exclamatione[2] dicens: " Dicis tu, inquit, si apparuerit dominus citra mare ? ymmo apparuit minus duodecim die*tis*[3] a loco ". [*Dixit frater Andreas : " Vbi fuit hoc ? " Respondit sanctus Egidius : " Quod vides vides ; quod audis, audis."*[4]] Dicit ei frater [Fol. 223 r.] Andreas :[5] " Bene inuenitur apparuisse dominus beato Petro prope Romam, in loco vbi dicitur ' Domine, quo vadis ' ". Respondit Frater Egidius : " Non dico de hoc, quia multum maius fuit hoc [*quod*] dico quam illud. Scio, inquit, talem locum citra mare[6] vbi fecit dominus maiora, quam vsquam fecerit citra mare alicui de hiis que ego audiui. Posse[*t*] dominus fecisse aliqua, que non audiui, sed de hiis que ego audiui, hoc fuit maius, quam fecerit humanitati." Dixit ei frater Andreas : " Magna fecit deus beato Petro Rome, beato Francisco Assisii, magna valde sunt hec que tu dicis, si sunt maiora illis ". Respondit frater Egidius : " Verum est, quod illa magna fuerunt, sed alia sunt opera dei & aliud est ipse "[7] & statim subiunxit " Oculi tui, domine, ammirabiles[8] & aures tue inenarrabiles. Alia tua sunt nimis magna." Dixit ei Frater Andreas : " Et vbi est locus iste ". Respondit sanctus Egidius : " Quod vides, vides & quod audis, audis ". Postea dixit : " Fuisti tu adhuc Clusii ? " ; dixit frater

---

[1] A. adds " Jesus Christus ".

[2] A. " Tunc statim respondit cum exclamatione magna ".

[3] MS. " diebus ".

[4] Supplied from A., taken in conjunction with S. and with L2, to fill an obvious accidental blank.

[5] So also S. and L2, but A. " Dixit etiam idem frater A.".

[6] A. omits " citra mare ".

[7] A. " aliud sunt opera Domini, aliud ipse Dominus ".

[8] A. " amabiles ".

14. Another time Brother Gratian his companion, and Brother James and Brother Andrew of Burgundy were with Saint Giles. Brother Gratian said to the aforesaid Brother Andrew : " It is found written in Holy Scripture that Our Lord should appear to one after His Resurrection on this side of the sea ". This he said, wishing to know of a truth whether Brother Giles would answer ought thereto. Saint Giles answered with earnestness : "Sayest thou that the Lord should appear on this side of the sea ? Yea verily, He appeared less than twelve days' journey from this spot." Brother Andrew said, " Where was that ? " Saint Giles answered : " What thou seest, thou seest ; what thou hearest, thou hearest ". Brother Andrew said unto him : " It is written of a truth that the Lord appeared to Blessed Peter near Rome, at the place which is called ' Domine, quo vadis ' ". Brother Giles answered : " I speak not of that, for that of which I speak was much greater than that. I know of a place on this side of the sea, where the Lord wrought greater things than any of which I have heard, which He ever wrought upon anyone on this side of the sea. It may be that the Lord has wrought some things of which I have not heard, but of those which I have heard, this was greater than He has ever before wrought among men." Brother Andrew said unto him : " God wrought great things upon Blessed Peter at Rome and upon Blessed Francis at Assisi : exceeding great must be the things of which thou speakest, if they are greater than those ". Brother Giles answered : " It is true that those were great things, but the works of God are one thing and God Himself another," and immediately he added : " Wondrous are Thine eyes, O Lord, and Thine ears past telling : the other parts of Thee are too great ! " Brother Andrew said unto him : " And where is that place ? " Saint Giles answered : " What thou seest, thou seest, and what thou hearest, thou hearest ". Afterwards he said : " Wast thou ever at Chiusi ? " " Nay," said Brother Andrew, " but I have

Andreas : " Non, sed vidi contratam illam " ; respondit sanctus Egidius dicens : " Bene," et subiunxit : " Scis tu quando facta sunt hec magna ? " Respondit Frater Andreas : " Et quando ? " Dixit sanctus Egidius : " Eo anno quo migrauit beatus Franciscus et duraverunt [1] a tertia die ante natiuitatem domini vsque ad vigiliam Epiphanie ". Dixit frater Andreas : " Durauit hoc factum, quod tu dicis tanto tempore continue vel interpellate ? " Respondit sanctus Egidius : " Non dico continue, sed per vices tantum fuit de die et de nocte ". Postea dixit : " Processi [2] multum in hiis verbis ". Dixit frater Andreas : " Credo, quod dominus vult, quod aliquando dicant serui sui aliqua secreta ad *vt*ilitatem [3] aliorum ". Respondit sanctus Egidius : " Non fuit in illo facto mea culpa ; multum enim rogaui tunc dominum & dixi ei quod non decebant [Fol. 223 v.] me ita magna. Sed ipse est dominus ; facit quod placet sibi."

15. Alia vice dixit Andreas sancto Egidio : " Magna fecit dominus in monte Aluerne beato Francisco ". Respondit sanctus Egidius : " Nescio talem montem citra mare, qualis est mons Pesulus ".[4] Dixit ei frater Andreas : " Nonne videtur tibi magnum valde, si angelus apparet alicui ? " Dixit ei sanctus Egidius : " Miror te, frater Andrea, quia [*si*] non esset celum et terra neque angeli neque archangeli neque aliqua creatura, non esset minor magnitudo dei propter hoc. Vnde hoc est magnum factum, quando apparet dominus." Dixit ei frater Andreas : " Vellem, quod fieret vna valde pulcra ecclesia, [*vbi fecit dominus ita magna* [5]]". Respondit sanctus Egidius : " Quam bene dicis ! " Dixit ei frater Andreas : " Quod vocabulum deberet [6] imponi illi ecclesie ? " Respondens sanctus Egidius : " Vocabulum festi Penthecostes ". Dixit ei frater Andreas : " Credis, quod spiritus sanctus ven*erit* [7] in aliquem postea, sicut venit in apostolis in die Penthecostes, hoc est in igne ? " Respondit sanctus Egidius : " Si ego glorifico meipsum,

---

[1] MS. adds " ante " which is superfluous.
[2] MS. " processit ".
[3] MS. " humilitatem ".
[4] A. " Pesulanus " ; L2 " Pessulus ".
[5] Supplied from A., S. and L2.
[6] A. adds " habere vel ".
[7] MS. " veniret ".

seen that land." Saint Giles answered, " Good," and added :
" Knowest thou when these great things were wrought ? "
Brother Andrew answered, " When ? " " In the year," answered
Saint Giles, "in which Blessed Francis was translated, and
they lasted from the third day before Our Lord's Nativity until
the Eve of the Epiphany." Brother Andrew said : " Did that
which was done of which thou speakest last continually for so
long a time or was it at intervals ? " Saint Giles answered :
" I say not continually, but now by day and now by night ".
Afterwards he said : "I have gone far in saying these words ".
Brother Andrew said : " I believe that it is the will of the Lord
that His servants should at times tell some of His secrets for
the edification of His people ". Saint Giles answered : "It
was no fault of mine that that deed was done : for I besought
the Lord much at that time and said unto Him, that so great
things became me not. But He is the Lord : He doeth what
seemeth to Him good."

15. Another time Andrew said to Saint Giles : " The
Lord wrought great things on Mount Alverna [1] upon Blessed
Francis ". Saint Giles answered : " I know of no mountain
on this side of the sea, which is so great as Mount Pesulus ". [2]
Brother Andrew said unto him : " Seemeth it not to thee an
exceeding great thing, that an angel should appear to any
man ? " Saint Giles said unto him : " I am astonished at thee,
brother Andrew, since if there were neither Heaven nor earth,
nor angels, nor archangels, nor any created thing at all, the
greatness of God would not be any the less on that account.
Wherefore it is a great thing indeed, when the Lord appears."
Brother Andrew said to him : " I would that an exceeding
beautiful church were built, where the Lord wrought so great
things ". Saint Giles answered : " Thou hast well said ! "
Brother Andrew said : " By what name should that church
be called ? " Saint Giles answering said : " By the name of the
feast of Pentecost ". Brother Andrew said to him : " Believest

[1] It was upon Mount Alverna in the Casentino that St. Francis in 1224
received the Stigmata.

[2] Mount Pesulus is near Cetona, the scene of B. Giles' great spiritual
experience.

gloria mea nichil est," et addit : " Non dicamus plus de ista
materia ".   O sancte Egydie et reuera sanctissime,[1] cui [*dominus*]
tantam gratiam [2] conferre dignatus est !   Ipse enim in persona
alterius de se ipso loquebatur dicens [3] : " Beatus Paulus, inquit,
[*dicitur*] [4] bis fuisse raptus, siue in corpore siue extra corpus,
adiungens : nescio, deus scit ; sed [*quid*] si aliquem dominus
certum redderet ".

15a. Moram [5] faciens aliquando sanctus Egidius apud
locum fratrum de Agello,[6] et [*cum*] hora consueta ad vesperas
vt cibum sumeret reuert*ere*tur,[7] ad fratres, post cenam fratribus,
qui [8] aderant ibi, verba domini plena dulcedine & deuotione non
modica incepit eructare : & talia sic proponens [Fol. 224 r.]
sancto ardens feruore fratrum audientium ardentia corda facit.
Et in tam sancto silentio et raptu [9] stetit coram fratribus quasi
vsque ad primum gallorum cantu[*m*].   Et [*erat*] clarissimum
lumen lune.   Cumque a fratribus [*discederet*] [10] et versus cellam
dirigeret gressus suos, subito tantus splendor aduenit quod lumen
lune ab illo totaliter est absor[*p*]tum. Quem fratres videntes sunt
non modicum stupefacti.   Ad quos rediens ipse sanctus Egidius,
quia parum [11] discesserat, dixit fratribus : " Quid fecissetis, si
vidissetis maiora ? "   Et adiecit : " Qui magna non videt, modica
magna credit ".   Et hiis dictis ad cellam vbi se celare[*t*] accessit.

Et quia demones sanctos viros et perfectos [12] non possunt
[*t*]erroribus nocere & molestare, ad aliam artem et tempta-
tiones confugiunt, videlicet superbie[*et*] vaneglorie.   Quodam

---

[1] C. and S. "sanctissimus".   [2] A. " gloriam ".
[3] A. " Etenim . . . de te ipso loquebaris ".   B. agrees with C.
[4] Supplied from S.
[5] The passage from this point to " reprehenderet " is not in A. or B. but is
in S.   It is found also in L2, pp. 106-107.
[6] MS. " Agnello ".   [7] MS. " revertitur ".
[8] MS. " quibus ".   [9] S. " Itaque, facto silentio, et raptus ".
[10] Supplied from S.   [11] MS. wrongly " patrum ".
[12] MS. here inserts " quibus," while S. inserts " quos," but neither appears
necessary.

thou that the Holy Spirit hath ever since come upon any one, as He came upon the Apostles on the day of Pentecost, that is in the form of tongues as of fire ? " Saint Giles answered : " If I honour myself, my honour is nothing," and added : " Let us speak no more of that matter ". O holy, yea indeed most holy Giles, upon whom the Lord was pleased to bestow so great grace ! He himself spoke thus concerning himself, as if speaking of another, saying : " Blessed Paul is said to have been twice caught up to heaven, either in the body or out of the body, adding ' I know not, God knoweth ' : but what, if God caused any man to know of a truth concerning this ? "

15a. When at one time Saint Giles was sojourning in the house of the Brethren at Agello[1] and when at the accustomed hour at vespers he returned to the brothers to partake of food, he began after supper to utter unto the brothers who were there divine words full of sweetness and of exceeding great devotion ; and as he thus poured forth these words, himself consumed with fervent zeal, he caused the hearts of the brothers who heard him to burn within them. And he remained in that holy silence and rapture before the brothers until the cock crew for the first time. And the light of the moon was exceeding bright. And when he departed from the brothers and made his way towards his cell, suddenly so great a light shone round about that the light of the moon was wholly eclipsed thereby. The brothers seeing this were exceeding astonied. But Saint Giles returning unto them, since he had gone but a little way, said unto them : " What would ye have done if ye had seen greater things ? " and added : " He who sees not great things, believes common things to be great ". And this said, he betook him to his cell to hide himself. And since the evil spirits are not able to hurt and trouble with their terrors holy men and perfect, they have recourse to other wiles and temptations, to wit pride and vainglory. At one time when he was in the place of Puppio and was standing praying in his cell one night, he heard the foul spirits standing beside him saying : " Why doth this man labour so hard ? Already he

---

[1] A place near Lake Trasimene in the district of Perugia.

tempore dum staret in loco de [*Puppio*],[1] stans in cella sua vbi orabat quadam nocte, audiuit demones stantes iuxta se dicentes : "Quid tantum laborat homo iste? Iam sanctus est. Iam vnctus[2] est. Iam exstaticus est." Ipse vero quesiuit postea a quodam socio suo, de quo multum confidebat, quid hoc esset, maxime de verbo "exstatico," quod non intelligebat. Cui ille respondit : "Ne cures, frater, quia dyabolica temptatio fuit".

Quodam tempore cum humilitate & caritate reprehenderet quemdam fratrem sanctus Egydius reprehensione dignum, frater ille dedignatus est. Cui in nocte sequenti astitit [*quidam*] in visione dicens ei :[3] "Ne indigneris, frater, in reprehensione sancti Egidii, quia beatus erit, qui credit ei". Mane autem facto [Fol. 224 v.] accessit frater ille ad sanctum Egidium, rogans eum ut secure eum reprehenderet.

16. Cumque iam ad diem appropinquaret sanctus Egidius obitu*s* su*i*,[4] vt dominus post laborem nimium & certamen requiem & coronam post victoriam[5] sibi daret, adhuc plus more solito cepit impugnari, vt probatus per omnia ostendatur. Nam cum quadam nocte post longas orationes quietem vellet facere post laborem corporis, demon cepit et in [*loco*] tam arto locauit, vt non posset aliquatenus[6] se mouere. Cumque sic existens anxietate maxima laboraret, vt surgeret, frater Gratianus sibi seruiens cepit aliquantulum hoc audire. Cumque vero magis celle appropinquaret, audiens clarius anxiantem fortiter, cum sic audiret, intra semetipsum cepit cogitare & dicere : "Si accedis propius et erit in oratione, ipsum orare permittas : sin autem aliter, videbis quid est". Et hiis dictis ad hostium celle iuit & cepit auscultare. Cumque sic audiret eum laborantem, alloquitur ipsum "Quid habes, frater?"[7] At ipse : "Veni, fili, veni !" Qui videns hostium et aperire non valens dixit : "Quid est, quod ego non pos-

---

[1] Supplied from S. But L2 reads "Prepo". See note 6, *Anal. Franc.*, III. p. 106.

[2] S. reads "victor," but L2 "unctus".

[3] MS. adds "Mane autem facto accessit frater ille," deleted.

[4] MS. "obitum suum". [5] A. omits "post victoriam".

[6] A. and L2 "aliquantulum". [7] A. "pater".

is holy. Already he hath an unction. Already he is ecstatic."
But afterwards he asked a certain companion whom he greatly
trusted, what this meant and chiefly concerning the word
"ecstatic," which he did not understand. His companion
answered him saying: "Heed it not, brother, for it was a
temptation of the devil".

It befell once that Saint Giles was with humility and love
admonishing a brother who was worthy of reproof, and the
brother was wrath. The following night there came unto
him one saying unto him: "Be not angry, brother, at the
reproof of Saint Giles, for he who believes him will be happy".
And when morning was come, the brother went to Saint Giles
and asked him to admonish him soundly.

16. Now when Saint Giles drew near to the day of his
death, in order that the Lord might give him rest after his
great toil and strife and a crown after victory, he began to be
assailed yet more than was his wont, so that he might be
proved in all things. For when one night after long prayers
he sought rest from his bodily toil, the devil seized him and
placed him in so narrow a place, that he could in no wise
move himself. And as he was striving with all his might to
lift himself up, Brother Gratian who was serving him, began
to hear sounds thereof. But approaching nearer to the cell,
he heard more distinctly how he was labouring hard, and
when he heard this he began to reflect thus within himself:
"If thou goest near and he is at prayer, thou wilt leave him
to pray: but if he be not so, thou wilt see what is amiss".
Having said which, he went to the door of the cell and began
to listen. And hearing him striving hard, he spoke to him
saying: "What ails thee, brother?" And he answered:
"Come hither, my son, come hither!" And seeing the door
and being unable to open it, he said: "Why is it that I cannot
open the door?" And Saint Giles answered: "Press, press
hard, my son, and thou shalt open the door! For I am
forced against the door by my foes and cannot rise." And

sum aperire?" Et sanctus Egidius: "Firma, firma, inquit, fortiter, fili, & hostium aperias [*velociter*.].[1] Nam [2] ego sum ab hostibus ostio ap[*p*]odiatus nec surgere possum;" qui et dum [*fortitudine adiutus*][3] impellens fortiter ostium aperuit violenter; intransque celle porticum, vbi sanctus Egidius iacebat, ipsum totis viribus erigere nitebatur & non valet erigere. Dixit sanctus Egidius: "Dimittamus in manu domini": quod ille, licet inuitus [*annuit*] sancto Egidio, & cum sic aliquantulum dimisisset, viriliter cepit ipsum et extraxit de loco illo *t*am [4] arto. Et postquam aliquantulum quieuisset [Fol. 225 r.] dixit socio suo: "Quare nititur tantum [5] dyabolus diuina beneficia impedire?" & ait socio suo: "Bene fecisti, inquit, fili, quod ad me venisti. Dominus, inquit, retribuat tibi." Et dixit ei socius suus: "Quare fecisti hoc, pater? cur me non vocabas? Qualem, inquit, conscientiam potuissemus habere, si tu mortuus fuisses, nam tibi et nobis reprehensibile valde fuisset." Cui sanctus Egidius respondit: "Quid tibi obest,[6] si fit vindicta de inimicis meis? quare sic [7] insidiatur dyabolus beneficiis dei? Et si semel hoc esset, portabile esset, et si bis vel ter vel iiij vel quinquies.[8] Sed scito pro firmo, quod quanto plus nititur molestare, tanto plus inferius descendit, quia resistit deo. [*Non enim, inquit, fuit meum principium servire deo*] sed dei; et finis erit simili modo propter misericordiam[*suam*]. Non [9] est mirum si demon tantum persequitur peccatorem, cum sciat ipsum de peccato natum et conceptum, quia videt eum ascendere ad locum illum vnde ipse cecidit. Nam sepius tribulauit et tribulat me, nec sinit me quiescere vllo modo."

17. Item, cum quadam nocte iuxta festum sancti Benedicti [10] sanctus Egidius orationem faceret ad dominum, demon

---

[1] MS. "violenter". So also S: but A "velociter".

[2] A. omits from "Nam . . . violenter". But B. agrees with C. substantially.

[3] MS. corrupt: reads "fortissime adiunctus".   [4] MS. "quam".

[5] MS. repeats "dixit socio suo".   [6] So also S.; A. omits "obest".

[7] A. "quare igitur inquit": S. "quare inquid . . . tantum".

[8] A. and L2 omit "vel iiij vel quinquies".

[9] A. omits whole sentence "Non . . . modo," but S. has it.

[10] S. agrees; A. and L2 omit "iuxta—Benedicti".

summoning all his strength he pushed with great force against the door and burst it open : and crossing the threshold of the cell, where Saint Giles lay, he strove with all his might to raise him up, but could not do so. Then said Saint Giles : "Let us leave ourselves in the hand of the Lord". And his companion, though unwillingly, consented unto Saint Giles, and when he had left him thus for a space, he seized him with all his strength and drew him out of that narrow place. And after he had rested awhile, he said to his companion : "Why doth the devil strive so hard to hinder the blessing of God? Thou didst well, my son, that thou camest to me. The Lord reward thee." And his companion said to him : "Why didst thou thus, my father? Why didst thou not call me? What conscience could we have had, if thou hadst been dead, for much blame would have fallen both upon thee and upon us." And Saint Giles answered : "What is it to thee, if my enemies revenge themselves upon me? Why doth the devil plot thus against the grace of God? And if this happened but once, it would be tolerable, or even if twice or thrice or four times or five times. But know of a truth, that the more he strives to hurt, so much the lower doth he fall, because he resisteth God. For it was not of my own will in the beginning that I served God, but through the will of God ; and so will the end be likewise through the mercy of God. It is no wonder that the devil thus persecutes a sinner when he knows that he is conceived and born in sin, for he sees the sinner rise to the very same place from which he himself fell. For often he troubled me and still troubleth me and suffereth me not any wise to rest."

17. Again upon a certain night about the time of the Feast of Saint Benedict,[1] while Saint Giles was praying unto the Lord, the devil sought to hinder the grace which was being ministered unto him of God. Being exceeding affrighted at the terror which the devil inspired, he began to cry aloud in his fear : "Help, brothers, help!" Brother Gratian who was in a cell near by, being aroused by his cries, rose up

---

[1] March 21st, i.e. about a month before B. Giles' death.

voluit se impedire beneficium a domino ministratum ; ad cuius terrorem valde perterritus, cepit terribilibus vocibus acclamare :[1] " Succurrite, fratres, succurrite ! " Ad quam vocem frater Gratianus excitatus, qui erat prope eum in quadam cella, velociter surrexit et iuit ad eum clamans fortiter et dicens : " Ne timeas, pater, ne timeas ! ego enim succurro tibi " ; & accedens ad cellam dixit : " Quid habuisti, pater ? " Qui dixit ei " Ne cures, fili, ne cures, fili ". Et frater patri respondit : " Dimitte me hic esse iuxta te, ex quo tantum te persequitur inimicus ". Cui dixit pater : " Dominus, inquit, retribuat tibi, fili : nam bene fecisti, quia ad me venisti. Vade, inquit, et reuertere ad locum tuum ". Ymmo [2] cum sero post comestionem [Fol. 225 v.] vellet redire ad cellam, dicebat : " In nocte exspecto martyrium ". Item cum quadam vice loqueretur cum quodam socio suo dixit : " A principio mundi vsque nunc melior religio nec expeditior religione fratrum minorum infra non apparuit ".

18. Cum sanctus Egidius maxime appropinquaret ad dies extremos,[3] cum reuerteretur a cella [4] gaudio indicibili cuidam socio suo dixit : " Fili, quid tibi videtur, quid sit hoc ? Ego inueni magnum thesaurum tam lucidissimum et splendidissimum, quod lingua carnea exprimi non valeret.[5] Ego deuasto, fili, ego deuasto. [Sed][6] dicas, fili, si benedicaris a deo, quid tibi videtur." Et sepius hoc iterabat ; tanto gaudio et ardore [7] erat enim cum hoc diceret repletus, quasi spiritu sancto ebrius videbatur. Cui cum quidam frater diceret, vt veniret et cibum sumeret, respondit " Hic est optimus cibus, fili " ; et frater quasi temptans eum respondit : " In talibus non est curandum, pater, veni, veni ut comedas ". Et sanctus non leuiter ferens responsum [8] dixit : " Non bene dixisti frater ; potius voluissem quod tam gravem alapam mihi

---

[1] A. " clamare et dicere ".

[2] So also S. to " apparuit " ; A. " cum autem vellet de sero post comestionem redire ad cellam, dicebat : Exspecto martyrium ".

[3] A. and B. " Cum esset prope obitum suum ". S. agrees with C.

[4] A., B., S., L2 " a cella " ; C. reads " ad cellam ".

[5] So also S. ; but A. " exprimere non possum ".   [6] MS. " Si ".

[7] So B. and S. ; but A. " odore ".   [8] MS. adds " et ".

quickly and went to him, crying out aloud: "Fear not, father, fear not, for I am coming to thy help". And coming to his cell he said: "What aileth thee, father?" And he replied: "Pay no heed, my son, pay no heed". And the brother answered: "Suffer me to stay here beside thee, since the enemy persecutes thee so sore". But the father said to him: "The Lord reward thee, my son; for thou didst well in that thou camest to me. Go, return to thine own place." And when at night he would return after supper to his cell, he would say, "I await my martyrdom this night". Again when once he was speaking with a certain companion he said: "From the foundation of the world until now no better Order nor more efficient hath been seen on earth than that of the Friars Minor".

18. When Saint Giles was drawing close to his last days, as he was returning from his cell he was filled with joy unspeakable, and said to a certain companion: "My son, how seemeth this unto thee? I have found a great treasure so glorious and magnificent, that it passeth mortal tongue to tell. I am troubled, my son, I am troubled.[1] But say, my son, if thou art blessed of God, how it seemeth to thee." And this he repeated oft: for when he spake thus, he was filled with such joy and zeal, that he seemed to be as it were drunk with the Holy Spirit. When a certain brother bade him come and partake of food, he answered: "This is the best food of all, my son". And the brother, as if to tempt him, answered: "For such things thou shouldest not care; come, father, come and eat". And the man of God, taking his answer in no spirit of lightness, said: "Thou spakest not well, brother; I would rather thou hadst smitten me hard enough upon the cheek to cause blood to flow". It may verily be believed that his

[1] The text is probably corrupt here. "Devasto" gives no good sense. "Devastor" is not much better, but might mean, "I am plagued or troubled". See Thes. Ling. Lat. under "devastor" (= vexare, concidere, conterere).

dedisses, quod sanguis exiuisset". Credendum est quod illa sanctissima anima iam sentiret, quod dilectus[1] [*suus*], sic[*ut*] locutus est sibi,[2] vellet extrahere [*eam*] de tabernaculo suo ad fruendum illum gloriosissimum [*thesaurum*] in celis, quem ab initio sue conuersionis meruit invenire, supererogare[3] et custodire. Nam illam mortem quam predixit [*et*] ex illo multo tempore desiderauit, ex hoc dominus adimpleuit desiderium suum.

19. Quadam enim vice cum quidam frater diceret eidem quod beatus Franciscus dixisset, quod seruus dei semper desiderare debet mori et finire morte martyrii, respondit sanctus Egidius di*cens*:[4] "Ego, inquit, nolo mori meliori morte quam de contemplatione". [Fol. 226 r.] Ymmo quodam tempore cum ex desiderio martyrii pro Christi amore iuit[5] ad Saracenos, postquam reuersus fuit et meruit ascendere ad culmen contemplationis,[6] ait: "Noluissem, inquit, tunc mori morte martyrii".

20. Prope obitum suum cepit fortiter febricitare et ex nimia anxietate tussis et dolore capitis et pectoris non poterat comedere & dormire nec quiescere. Sed super lectum fratres die noctuque portabant ipsum, vt quietem inueniret. [*In*] vigilia vero sancti Georgii martyris nocte illa hora matutinali cum fratres sic ipsum super lectum portarent, posuerunt caput eius super lectum, et sic quasi videbatur quiescere sine tractu clausis oculis et ore tunc rapta est illa sanctissima anima ad supernam patriam transmissa.

O sancte Egidie et reuera sanctissime, qui eodem die, quo dominus te inspirauit et adduxit ad beatum Franciscum, vt imitare[*ri*]s eum, & ipse illo die te induit vestimento religionis, reuolutis quinquaginta duobus annis, illo eodem die dominus te perduxit ad ciuitatem ciuium supernorum!

Quedam persona sancta vidit per visionem, quod dominus cum militia angelorum et animarum sanctarum obuiauit et

---

[1] MS. "frater" instead of "suus".
[2] A. omits "sicut . . . sibi".
[3] So S.; A. omits "supererogare".
[4] MS. "dixit"; S. "dicens".
[5] A. "iuerat"; S. and B. "iuerit".   [6] MS. "et".

most holy soul already perceived that his Beloved, as he himself said, sought to draw it forth from its earthly tabernacle to enjoy that most glorious treasure in the heavens, which from the beginning of his conversion he was counted worthy to find and guard : for the Lord fulfilled his longing by granting unto him that very death which he foretold and which he so long desired.

19. When once a certain brother said to him that Blessed Francis had said that the servant of God ought always to desire to die and to meet a martyr's death, Saint Giles answered saying : " I desire to die no better death than that of contemplation ". And when at a certain time out of a desire to suffer martyrdom for the love of Christ he went to the Saracens and having returned thence was counted worthy to ascend to the very height of contemplation, he said : " I am glad that I did not then die a martyr's death ".

20. As his death drew near, he fell into a high fever, and by reason of wracking cough and pain in head and chest he could neither eat nor sleep nor rest. But the brothers bore him in their arms day and night upon his bed, to help him to find rest. On the eve of the Feast of Saint George the Martyr, at the hour of the night office while the brothers were thus bearing him, they laid his head on his couch and so he seemed to be resting with eyes and mouth closed and without drawing of breath : and then his most holy soul was caught up to its home in heaven above.

O most holy Giles, who on the self same day upon which the Lord inspired thee and led thee to Blessed Francis to follow after him and on which he himself clothed thee with the garb of religion, fifty and two years afterwards, wast brought by the Lord into the fellowship of the Citizens of Heaven !

In the year when he was translated to Heaven a certain holy man beheld in a vision how the Lord with a great company of angels and holy souls went to meet him and received him in the air and caught him up with honour and with angelic songs.

occurrit illi in aer*e*[1] anno quo celum ascenderet[2] et cum honore et cantico angelorum assumpsit eum.

21. Septem valde laudabilia et salutaria et perfecta[3] habuit in se sanctus Egydius: a primordio[4] conuersionis sue & cottidie vsque ad diem mortis magis ac magis perfecti*or*[5] [*extitit*][6] propter que creditur quod dominus larga sue benedictionis manu[7] graciam suam multiplicasset in eo et donis eum potioribus ampliasset.[8] Primum quod fidelissimus & catholicus fuit: secundum, deuotus: tertio, reuerens: quarto, pius & compatiens: quinto, sollicitus: sexto, obediens: septimo gratissimus deo et hominibus fuit de beneficiis sibi collatis.

EXPLICIT VITA BEATI EGIDII QUAM COMPOSUIT FRATER LEO ET SCRIPSIT PROPRIA MANU. DEO LAUS SEMPER. ANNO M CCCC XXXVIIJ IN VIGILIA ASCENSIONIS.

[1] MS. aera. So also A, B, and S.—a very peculiar form and a good example of the close connection between these MSS.

[2] So S.; A. and B. omit " anno . . . ascenderet ".

[3] So S.; A. omits " et perfecta ".   [4] A. " principio ".

[5] MS. " perfectium ".   [6] Supplied from A.

[7] MS. " largam . . . manum ".   [8] MS. " amplicasset ".

21. Saint Giles possessed seven exceeding laudable, wholesome, and perfect qualities : from the beginning of his conversion and daily until his dying day he became more and more perfect, wherefore it is believed that the Lord multiplied His grace upon him with a bounteous hand and caused him to abound with even mightier gifts.   First, that he was most believing and most loyal to the Catholic Faith : second, devout : third, reverent : fourth, pious and compassionate : fifth, zealous : sixth, obedient : seventh, beloved of God and men by reason of the virtues which joined themselves in him. ·

HERE ENDETH THE LIFE OF BLESSED GILES WHICH BROTHER LEO COMPOSED AND WROTE WITH HIS OWN HAND.   PRAISE BE TO GOD ALWAYS.   IN THE YEAR 1438 ON THE EVE OF THE ASCENSION.

APPENDIX.

BIBLIOGRAPHY.

THE following list aims merely at indicating the principal works bearing upon Blessed Giles of Assisi. It would have to be largely extended if it were to include all the works bearing upon the critical problems discussed in the Introduction.

Acta Sanctorum, April, tom. iii., pp. 222-249. 1866.

Actus Beati Francisci et Sociorum Ejus. Ed. by P. Sabatier. Collection d'Etudes, vol. iv. 1902.

Bartholomew of Pisa : *De Conformitate Vitae B. Francisci ad Vitam Domini Jesu. Analecta Franciscana,* tom. iv., pp. 205-233 and *passim.* Quaracchi. 1906.

Bulletti, Fr. Henry. *De Vita B. Ægidii Assisiensis auctore Fr. Leone. Archivum Franciscanum Historicum,* fasc. i-ii. 1915.

Celano, Thomas of. *S. Francisci Assisiensis Vita et Miracula.* Ed. by P. Ed. d'Alençon. Rome, 1906.

Chronica XXIV Generalium. Analecta Franciscana, tom. ii., pp. 74-115. Quaracchi. 1897.

Dicta Beati Ægidii Assisiensis. Quaracchi. 1905.

Documenta Antiqua Franciscana. Ed. by L. Lemmens.

    Pars I. *Scripta Fratris Leonis.* Quaracchi. 1901.

    Pars III. *Extractiones de Legenda Antiqua.* Quaracchi. 1902.

Fratini, Fr. Giuseppe. *Vita del B. Egidio D'Assisi.* Assisi, 1898.

Goetz, Prof. Walter. *Die Quellen zur Geschichte des hl. Franz von Assisi.* Gotha, 1904.

La Leggenda di San Francesco scritta da tre suoi Compagni. Ed. by Marcellino da Civezza and Teofilo Domenichelli. Rome, 1899.

Lives of the Saints and Blessed of the Three Orders of St. Francis, vol. ii., pp. 89-100.   Taunton.

Macdonell, Anne.   *Sons of Francis*, pp. 51-79.   London, 1902.

Menge, Fr. Gisbert.   *Der Selige Ægidius von Assisi. Sein Leben und Seine Sprüche.*   Paderborn, 1906.

Robinson, Fr. Paschal.   *The Golden Sayings of Brother Giles of Assisi.*   Philadelphia, 1907.

INDEX.